MW01102317

And the Sun Stood Still

See it the Way it Really Is— Faith In 3-D

Guy Parrish

PRESS

Xulon Press
10640 Main Street
Suite 204
Fairfax, VA 22030
(703) 934-4411
XulonPress.com

To order additional copies, call 1-866-909-BOOK (2665).

Acknowledgments

I want to acknowledge, with great gratitude and thanks, all the people who helped make my dream a reality.

To Keleta my wife – Thank you for your unbelievable love, help and encouragement. I could have never finished this project without your support. To be honest, I can't do anything without you. What a blessing you are! Darling, I love you so much!

To my secretary Pam Jones - Who so patiently typed, proofed, checked and rechecked. The hours you have spent will never be forgotten. Thanks for your tireless efforts. You are the best!

To Clifford Hurst – For over 20 years we have been friends. You have helped me in so many ways to be a better communicator. Your friendship has been one of the rewards of my ministerial life. Thanks for your keen sense and sharp mind. I trust you with my life.

To Gene Speck – You have been a true friend and faithful supporter. You always believe in me and make me feel more effective than I really am. Thank you for all you have done in helping me get this book published; it's been incredible! I wish everyone thought as highly of me as you do.

To Betty Gore – I am so grateful for your attention to detail, insightful observations, and suggestions. Your endeavor was the icing on the cake.

To the faithful and loving congregation of Central Assembly of God in Muskogee, Oklahoma - You have been the greatest people in the world. You have made pastoring a joy instead of a burden. Every day you make my dreams come true. You encourage me more than I could ever encourage you.

To my board – You are my friends and as friends you have restored my faith in leadership in a time when I was down. Yes, pastor/board relationships really do work. You're a gift from God.

To my staff – You are true armor bearers and I am proud you are on my team.

To Steve Radanovich – Thanks a million for your generous gift. The note book computer is a life saver. I am so glad I have a friend like you that has vision.

To my three wonderful kids, Silas, Shanta and Simeon – The apple of my eye is you. You make my life worth living!

To my mother Sherri – You have always believed in your son even when no one else did. I am not ashamed to admit I am still a momma's boy. Mom, I love you!

To my father Sim (Buzz) – Who has taught me a lot about life. You have placed things in my character that makes me eternally grateful. I love you!

To my father and mother-in- law Harvey and Ina Brown – Thank you for allowing me to marry your daughter. You have been like a father and mother to me. I never dreamed a mother in law could be so wonderful. You are absolutely the best! Harvey you are one of the most inspiring preachers I have ever known. You are the wisest man I know and with you as my father-in-law, I am blessed!

To my brothers Tim (my big brother and hero all my life) and Todd (my little brother, the preacher) and to my only sister Tonya – Thank you for following me in the faith. You have inspired me and taken a big burden off my life. God blessed me with you.

To Wayne Morrow – A friend, a brother and a mentor. I have never known a more dynamic minister of the gospel. You have given me a goal to reach and have inspired my ministry like no other preacher. It has been my privilege to be so close to someone so great.

To Tim Smith – You are a real friend and I can always count on you. Thanks for listening to my thoughts and lending your tremendous insight. I guess we are as close as you get as friends without being blood brothers. You are a prince of a friend and preacher.

To Timmy Williams – I have never met another person like you any where on this earth. You are a real blessing to me. Your encouragement to write this book has been amazing.

This volume
is affectionately dedicated
to my wife

Keleta Shanta,

the best friend I've ever had,
a faithful helpmeet in all
the cares of my life & ministry,
and whose love, support and dedication to me
have been phenomenal.

Contents

Chapter

1

And the Sun Stood Still

Then spake Joshua to the LORD in the day when the LORD delivered up the Amorites before the children of Israel, and he said in the sight of Israel, Sun, stand thou still upon Gibeon; and thou, Moon, in the valley of Ajalon. And the sun stood still, and the moon stayed, until the people had avenged themselves upon their enemies.
Joshua 10:12-13

And Jesus stood still.
Mark 10:49

*D*o you ever have enough time? In our attempt to regain paradise lost, the human mind has created a ton of timesaving devices. With our microwaves, jet planes, cell phones, fax machines, super highways, and, now, the almighty Internet we should slow the pace to low gear. There ought to be enough time to burn, but there's not. I heard a funny little story that relates to time and the saving of it. An efficiency expert was driving through the countryside when he noticed an old farmer in a pear orchard feeding his pig. What he saw drove him absolutely crazy, for the farmer was holding the pig over his head and moving him from pear to pear in the trees while the pig ate with a smile. The efficiency expert turned around, parked, and walked up to the farmer, saying, "Hey, there, old-timer, have I got a good idea for you." The farmer asked him what it was and the expert continued, "Just put the pig on the ground, get a stick, knock the pears to the ground, and let the pig eat them off the ground. It sure will save a lot of time." The old farmer thought about this for a moment, moved his pig to another pear and finally said, "Aw shucks, mister, what's time to a pig?" Honestly, pigs have no perception of time but people do and time is more valuable than money.

At this very moment it is 6:23 A.M. and I have been in my office since 4:00 A.M. It's not in my daily schedule to get up with the chickens. As a matter of fact, I usually come home with the cows. But I went to bed fairly early last night, around 11:30 P.M., and I woke up at 2:00 A.M. I couldn't go back to sleep. All I could do was lie there and think of all the things I had on my agenda for the day. So I got up, showered, and started my routine. As I came out of my house, I was met by Robert Bryan, who delivers our paper and attends our church. He got out of his car and we struck up a conversation which went something like this.

"Are you going to the hospital, Pastor?"

"No," I replied. "I am going to church."

"What church?" he asked.

I figured he asked that because besides pastoring a great church, I am frequently invited to speak at other churches.

"Our church."

"Why our church?" he asked. "Is there a problem?"

I quickly set his mind at ease and explained to him my temporary sleeping disorder.

"I have so much to do that it made more sense to me to get up and begin my work rather than lie there thinking about it, staring up at the shadowy, dark ceiling." I said.

Now, if history repeats itself, as it normally does, when I do finally come home with the cows tonight, I will not have finished every task. Life at its slowest is still an escalating rat race and the rats are winning. To compound the problem, we are equipped with all the latest technological break-throughs in the categories of minute economizing or time saving. We are always in a hurry, even if we don't have any place to go. Some people are in such a rush that when they pull up to a drive-thru car wash they are looking for the passing lane. They pray someone will one day invent instant instant coffee. There just doesn't seem to be enough hours in the day.

This was Joshua's dilemma, time was running out. Five Kings of the Amorites had conspired together to destroy the city of Gibeon because they were mighty men and it was a great city. That city had made peace with Joshua, and they were now Israel's allies. The five kings gathered with their armies around Gibeon. As the sun began to make its voyage to the other side of the earth, destruction seemed imminent. There was one small flicker of hope. These people knew if Joshua showed up, God would show up. So, they dispatched an envoy at lightning speed with this message:

Dear Joshua,

HELP!!! NOW!!! We have a problem!
Get here quick, like yesterday, and save us!
We've got 5 bad boys encamped outside our city.

Yours truly,
your old buddies,
The city of Gibeon

After Joshua read the desperate SOS, the Lord spoke to him and said, "Fear them not: for I have delivered them into thine hand; there shall not a man of them stand before thee," (Joshua 10:8). Joshua and his army traveled all night, and in the morning they caught the enemy by surprise. As they clashed in battle, the Lord threw the Amorites into a panic, and they broke the lines and ran in every direction. With the help of the Lord Himself, Joshua began to slaughter the enemy of God with the sharpened sword. And, as if that wasn't enough, God rained down hailstones from heaven; in fact, more men died from the hailstorm than from the swords' edge. But, as the shadows lengthened, Joshua knew the twilight was not far behind. He was running out of time. Though victory was no doubt won that day, the total victory would be lost at the setting of the sun. I am sure he thought to himself, "I've got the enemy on the run, and, if I wait until tomorrow, there is that possibility that they will regroup, and we may be forced to take a defensive position. If I only had a little more time, we could terminate and completely annihilate this enemy." At that pivotal point there came to his heart a frightening but most fascinating thought, "Just stop the universe until you win!" I believe everything in hell rebelled against that. Spirits of doubt and unbelief zeroed in on Joshua and offered every excuse and reason why this was not just impossible but ludicrous to the core. I can hear voices offering strong delusion, "Joshua, get hold of yourself. You must be weary from the battle. It's true you are God's man, but you're not God. Only a fool or lunatic would even contrive such a ridiculous thought." But, Joshua cast away every evil suggestion and held onto the faith of God that was placed in his heart. He then turned his head toward heaven and prayed loud enough that all of Israel heard, "God, please make the sun stand still!" Then suddenly the unthinkable, unbelievable, yet irrefutable miracle happened, and there is recorded a day in history that the sun stood still! Joshua spurred his horse and chased the enemy down to the man. The sun never moved, flinched or blinked an eye until Joshua and his mighty men avenged themselves upon their enemies. "So the sun stood still in the midst of heaven, and hasted not to go down about a whole day," (Joshua 10:13).

You can make the sun stand still. I know what you are thinking, "Where is he coming from? I am no Joshua!" Guess what? God knows that, and you don't have to be. You just have to be you. "The effectual fervent prayer of a righteous man availeth much," (James 5:16).

There once lived an old bootlegger just outside of town and on the river in the grand ole southern state of Mississippi. His mother gave him his name, Joshua. His daddy gave him his occupation, moonshiner. In jest he was asked one day by a potential customer, "Are you the Joshua that made the sun stand still?" And he replied in his back-woodsy brogue, "No, sir, I's the Joshua that made the moonshine still!"

You don't have to be Joshua, but you do have to be saved and qualify to be righteous for God to hear your prayer. Faith, righteousness, and prayer are a tri-fold cord that cannot be broken. With God's help you can move any obstacle in the universe.

We are quick to believe in miracles for others, but somehow when it comes to us personally, faith seems to wane on the ragged edge. You believe David did kill the giant, but you don't believe you can kill any giants. You believe the three Hebrew boys came out of the fiery furnace alive, but you don't believe you'll come through your fiery ordeal. You truly believe Daniel spent all night in a den of lions, but you just can't seem to believe that God will protect you from what has desire to eat you up. If you believe Joshua made the sun stand still, believe you can do the same. It is not enough to believe with your brain that God will do miracles; you must believe it with your heart that God will do it for you. The Lord doesn't answer prayer on the merit of skin color, social status or financial capital. God answers prayer on the value of your right standing with Him and your faith in Him.

Somewhere in the pursuit for spiritual elitism we have lost the "wonder" of God. We have made Christianity predictable. I like the prayer of one old saint who prayed "God will you please do something that is not in the bulletin today!" The Spirit of God is unpredictable. He is like the wind. "The wind bloweth where it listeth, and thou hearest the sound thereof, but canst not tell whence it cometh, and whither it goeth: so is every one that is born of the Spirit," (John 3:8). Where has the "wonder" of God gone, that high level of expectancy that dared to believe God for anything? Perhaps we have prayed so many prayers that seemingly never received an answer that now we look at what we would call a hopeless situation and our attitude is, "Well, I know God could do it, but I seriously don't believe He will." We have allowed our hearts to get so calloused until our faith has lost its luster. The Bible has become just a good example instead of a wonderful experience. We have reduced prayer down to just a dead ritual, and most churches are business as usual.

The rallying point and faith cry of the battle that should resound from every blood-bought believer is, "Our God is able!" After all, at God's command the world was set in space and sent spinning on its axis at one thousand miles per hour and the oceans have never lost one drop. He stretched the blue canopy of heaven overhead and then flung the twinkling stars against the nocturnal sky. He traced out the rivers with His majestic finger and scooped out the mighty channels of the deep with His omnipotent hand. He pushed the valleys down and bowed the mountains up. He hung the sun and the moon out as golden and silver chandeliers. Our God is able! The Apostle took out his prophetic pen and inscribed the testimony of God for every generation to believe, "Now unto him that is able to do exceeding abundantly above all that we ask or think, according to the power that worketh in us," (Ephesians 3:20).

You may say, "That sounds good, but I've tried to pray and it just doesn't seem to work." Have you ever flipped the light switch and the lights didn't come on? Did you conclude that it is just not the will of electricity to light a light bulb? Or did you think that maybe electricity had something against you, and although it lights the neighbor's house, there is no indication that it will do the same for you. After all, you are not in its inner circle! To be quite frank, I don't think electricity really likes you so just forget it and learn to live in the dark. I mean this with all respect, I don't believe anyone is that naive. There must be a reasonable and normal explanation, and there is. Let me offer four possibilities:

1. A broken switch;
2. A bad connection;
3. A blown fuse;
4. A burned out bulb.

So you prayed and didn't receive an answer—at least that was your perception—and you concluded that prayer either doesn't work or God just doesn't care. You probably told yourself, "It doesn't do any good to pray because I have no favor with God." But the Bible tells us opposite. God does care and prayer changes things. If your prayers have not been answered, you need to do a little troubleshooting and find the real cause. Again, look at four possibilities:

1. A broken switch—A broken relationship with God, like Saul who backslid and left the Lord out of his decisions.
2. A bad connection—Wrong attitudes in your life, like the Pharisee in the temple who didn't leave justified.
3. A blown fuse—Sin in your life, like Samson, robs you of all spiritual power.
4. A burned out bulb—Burned out faith, like Solomon who became the wisest fool in the Bible.

The fervent prayer of a righteous person really works because God works, and when God works miracles happen. Prayer is not a ritual, and it is so much more than rosary beads or a prayer wheel. It's not dead ritualistic repetitious mumbo-jumbo that some Christians have prayed a thousand times. Prayer is a hotline to heaven; it's talking to God and letting God talk to you. There is no problem too big for God if you will pray.

After the Bolshevik Revolution, a Communist soldier caught a Christian peasant praying and in an intimidating way asked, "Who are you praying for?" The peasant replied, "Well, sir, I'm praying for Lenin." The soldier then asked, "Well, I suppose you prayed for the Czar as well when he was in power?" Peasant: "Yes, sir, I did." And the soldier responded with a sarcastic tone, "I guess you know what happened to the Czar?" The peasant, with a sly grin, said, "Exactly!"

Has it ever occurred to you that Joshua is not the only man

in the Bible that made the sun stand still? Blind Bartimaeus was on the roadside begging when he heard that Jesus was coming right by him. He began to cry out and say, "Son of David, have mercy on me." He, like Joshua, faced a similar impediment. Time was running out. The only difference is that in Joshua's case, the darkness was coming; in the blind man's case the darkness was already there and had been there all his life. As far as Bartimaeus was concerned, Jesus may never come that way again. The planetary sun is God's lamp that lights the world. Jesus proclaimed in no uncertain terms, "I am the light of the world: he that followeth me shall not walk in darkness, but shall have the light of life," (John 8:12). Both men were in a battle and both had the daring faith to believe that all things are possible. Just like Joshua, every doubt and unbelief tried to derail this poor blind man in his pursuit for the miracles of God. Those around Bartimaeus told him to hold his peace, in other words, "Shut up!" But perhaps in the hidden resources of his mind he remembered that Joshua made the sun stand still though he had never witnessed with his eyes the setting or the rising of the sun. This marvelous revelation was revealed to his heart; he too could make the sun stand still. Then, like the turning on of a light bulb, the prophecy of that great prophet Malachi was revealed to him: "But unto you that fear my name shall the **Sun of righteousness** arise with healing in his wings," (Malachi 4:2). So, instead of cowering to the pressure, the Bible says he cried even louder. Again, as with Joshua, he prayed loud enough that all of Israel heard him that day, and it is recorded in time that a second man made the Sun stand still! "And Jesus stood still," (Mark 10:49).

We often let circumstance, trouble, and doubt eclipse God. Do you know how big the sun is? Picture this: You could pour one million three hundred thousand earths into the sun. The earth is eighty-one times larger than the moon. You could pour one hundred five million moons into the sun. With these colossal statistics in mind, how can the moon eclipse the sun? Simple: Because of distance. The moon is two hundred thirty-eight thousand miles from earth. The sun is ninety-three million miles from earth. If you were to drive to the sun at the speed of sixty-five miles per hour, nonstop, it would take one hundred sixty-three years to get there. The moon is much closer to the earth. Why do doubt, fear, and trouble seem to loom bigger on the horizons of our life? Because we are often standing closer to the mountain than to the Maker. Draw near to God. Draw near in faith, in prayer, and the things of this earth will grow strangely dim in the light of His glory and grace.

Don't let unbelief and doubt keep you from the miracle. Whatever you need at whatever time you need it, Jesus is available. Pray and call on the Lord; He controls time. He extended it for Hezekiah, rolled back the sundial of Ahaz, and He stopped it for Joshua. Time doesn't get the best of Jesus because He invented time. The word "immediately," which is a matter of time, is associated with most of our Lord's miracles. "And Jesus said unto Bartimaeus, go thy way; thy faith hath made thee whole. And immediately he received his sight, and followed Jesus in the way," (Mark 10:52). Jesus is only a prayer away. Always remember, Jesus is never a moment too early, and He is never a moment too late, He is always right on time.

Chapter
2

The Rose Will Bloom Again

The wilderness and the solitary place shall be glad for them; and the desert shall rejoice, and blossom as the rose.
Isaiah 35:1

A jewelry salesman from Fresno, California drove to Santiago in hopes of making a sale. He was hard pressed by some personal problems that had developed in his life. That one of his sample cases was stolen in Phoenix, Arizona gave his optimism a deadly blow. Upon arrival in Santiago, he got a room in a hotel near a big shopping center. He then drove around the block, parked his car in the parking lot of the shopping center, went in, and was unsuccessful in presenting his product. When he came out of the retail store and found his car and all his possessions were stolen (over one hundred thousand dollars in value), it was just too much for him. His camel's back was one straw away from breaking down, and this was it. He walked back to his hotel and took the elevator to the fifth floor. Then he walked out on the balcony that overlooked the inside of the building, climbed over the rail and plunged to his death. There is a sad twist to this story: He merely forgot where he had parked his car. His car and all his possessions were in the parking lot the whole time.

Here is a man much like you and I. He had everything to live for, yet hopelessness pushed him over the edge. People don't get discouraged just because bad things happen to good people. We have a universal understanding of pain and discouragement that has been hammered into the fabric of our psyche through the duration of many millenniums. What carpenter has not hit his thumb in the process of driving his nails? What parent has not suffered heartache in the process of rearing children? What Christian has not suffered the darkness of Gethsemane all alone? We all have, and we all will, so we can deal with that. But when people lose hope, they give up on life. When they can't see a bright tomorrow, they give up on today, and they are swallowed up in the darkness of defeat. If you, by the power of persuasion, can convince a man that he has no hope, he will curse the day he was born.

Hope is the indispensable quality of life. It is the oil that greases the gears of human machinery in spite of a grueling pace. But, sad to say, many people in this world have lost their hope. They have given up on their health, their marriage, their finance, and a thousand other things too numerable to list. Hope is the exciting expectation or anticipation that God is getting ready to do something out of the ordinary just for you!

But for many, hope has faded like a good dream not to be remembered. Hope has drained like the dew from the fragrant rose under the heat of the mid-morning sun. What was, not so long ago an oasis of green, luscious grass is now a barren, tormented dessert. Hopelessness is represented by the desolate desert where the heat rises to one hundred twenty degrees in the shade, but there is no shade; where the ground breaks open like dehydrated and thirsty lips praying for rain; where, when you need water, you can only find sand; where, when you need food, you can only find the towering cactus armed for protection against all predators. Companionship is reduced to wild coyotes, slithering rattlesnakes, and tumbleweeds. Dust devils are as common as pictures at a family reunion. The desert is a lonely, hot, dry, and dangerous place. But, out of this hopelessness God said, "I will cause the rose to emerge." There is no situation too hopeless, no desert too dry that the rose can't bloom again! Don't lose hope in God, for He has not nor will He ever let you down.

One night as my family and I were watching television and I was surfing through the channels, I came upon an opera. I will be the first to admit opera is not my style of singing. But there was just something that I had to know, so much to the annoyance to my family every few minutes I would hit the previous channel on my remote. With only a few minutes left in the concert it happened. The curtain opened and a beautiful woman who weighed in excess of four hundred pounds appeared. We sat and watched her flawless performance until the end of the program, and as the credits descended from the top of the screen, I came up off of the couch from where I was lying, pointed my finger at the television and shouted "It's true, it's true, it's true." My wife asked "What is true?" I replied "The opera ain't over 'til the fat lady sings!"

There is another old saying, "It's not over till it's over." We can add, "It's not over till God says it's over." And with God it is never over. Amos, Chapter 3, tells how the lion stole a little lamb. When the shepherd got to the lion's lair, he slew the beast and took from his mouth the only thing left of the lamb, "two legs and a piece of ear." With this one verse God illustrates how if there is nothing left but two legs and a piece of ear, He can bring to life that which is dead. If Jesus Christ can resurrect hope with only two legs and a piece of ear, face your circumstance with confidence of soul. Step into your personalized arena of battle with full assurance of faith. Walk back into your business, back into your marriage, with a heart full of hope and say, "If God can restore that little lamb with nothing but two legs and a piece of ear, He can put my life back together again."

The Bible is full of articulation of hope out of hopelessness. There is a golden thread that is woven throughout its divine pages called hope. After the fall of man iniquity reached an all time zenith, and it repented the Lord that He even made man. "But Noah found grace in the eyes of the Lord." He built an ark at God's command. The rains came and Noah and his family rode the storm out for forty days and forty nights. There were dark nights and long days. The whole world was a watery grave. Then one day the ark landed. Noah and his family of seven emerged into the sunshine to start civilization over again. Before the flood earth was a barren desert of sin, but God washed it clean with the waters of His own judgment. The desert rejoiced, and the rose bloomed again.

In the final two verses of the final book of the Old Testament God said, "Behold, I will send you Elijah the prophet before the coming of the great and dreadful day of the Lord: And he shall turn the heart of the fathers to the children, and the heart of the children to their fathers, lest I come and smite the earth with a curse," (Malachi 4:5-6). Turn only one page to the first verse of the first chapter of the New Testament, and it says, "The book of the generation of Jesus Christ, the son of David, the son of Abraham," (Matthew 1:1). You just skipped four hundred years. For four centuries heaven was brass. There was no word, no wonder, no vision or voice. It was a time of silent hopelessness; not a prophet was stirring, no, not even a preacher was in the house. But after one hundred and forty-six thousand days of prophetic silence, "There was a man sent from God, whose name was John," (John 1:6). And with a fiery proclamation he rent the air like a silver trumpet, "Repent for the kingdom of God is at hand, hope is on the horizon the Lord has come!" The silence was broken and the rose bloomed again.

You may feel at times that God has released the devil on you, but the reality is God has released you on the devil. The only way you and I can be defeated is to walk away from God. We are gabled to the throne, and, if you think evil is going to submerge God, you've missed it a million miles. There is no depth to hell on this earth that God will not empty, if you'll just ask Him to.

When Satan throws you into a crisis, it only means one thing: You have not been conquered. The enemy is not attacking the old, dead, lame, do-nothing-but-sit-on-a pew-kind of church member. He has them already. They are sound asleep and have been brought under his power, and he is not worried about those that he already has. Ask any duck hunter; it is not the dead ducks that are already in the boat that occupy them, it is the live ones that fly overhead. If you are alive and filled with God's resurrection power, Satan is going to do everything within his schemes to bring you down. So his attack upon your life means you're still alive and you have not been defeated. Maybe no one knows the battle that rages in your life, the tears, fears and hopelessness that invades the tranquility of your mind. Negative forces have gathered outside the outer limits of your happiness. Suicide may even seem to have its advantages. You are under attack, so pick your head up and shout "hallelujah" because you are still winning. Satan is trying your faith and that is a sign that you have not been defeated. Hell has taken its best shot against your faith and you have fallen down, but you just keep getting back up. You may be down at times, but you are never out. God still has a plan. It's called resurrection. It is like the power of a small cork in the middle of vast ocean. Try as the ocean will to submerge the cork, it always comes back to the surface. Faith will keep you afloat because it has buoyancy.

The word buoyancy has several definitions, among them

"lightness or resilience of spirit." Trouble always exposes what you are made of. If you are a Christian you are made out of the right stuff.

> "A little brown cork
> Fell in the path of a whale
> Who lashed it down
> With his angry tail.
> But in spite of its blows
> It quickly arose,
> And floated serenely
> Before his nose.
> Said the cork to the whale:
> 'You may flap and sputter and frown
> But you never, never, can keep me down,
> For I'm made of the stuff
> That is buoyant enough
> To float instead of to drown!'"

> —Author Unknown

Don't lie down and give up. Never say die. If you have only a little wiggle in your finger or a small quiver in your toe, you are still alive and the enemy has not vanquished you. Christ's resurrection makes you more than a conqueror. Jesus Christ has proven mastery over every enemy of life and wants you mastered by nothing but Him. Yet we are faced with a most disappointing truth: Many are not living in such victory. In spite of every tangible promise of God, countless Christians are whipped by life. Though they desperately struggle, in the final analysis, disillusionment and distress seem to be the order of the day. Like a fly caught in a web, the more they struggle it becomes apparent their liberty is non-existent. But it doesn't have to be that way. You are not the victim. You are the victorious! Jesus Christ who conquered the last fortress on the frontier of life, who for our sakes went to the grave and beyond, came back to tell us, "I am He that liveth, and was dead; and, behold, I am alive for evermore, Amen; and have the keys of hell and of death," (Revelation 1:18). Sometimes you wonder why the devil is so angry. He doesn't even have the key to his own front door because Jesus stripped him of all his keys. Who wouldn't be upset and totally frustrated? You may be living in what you call hell on this earth. But He has the key to your personal hell. He has the key to your sickness, to your trouble, to your material problem, to your storm, and your rose can bloom again.

Learn the parable of the wasp and spider: It happened one hot summer day in the Lone Star State, Texas. We were there on a visit to see my mother and father-in-law. Just as I stepped out the front door a small stirring in the corner of the porch arrested my attention. A very small spider had lured and caught a red wasp in his sticky web. The wasp was at least four times the size of the spider, but the web had him subdued. After a long struggle the battle was over and the wasp gave up and just resigned to its fate. The spider got up as to flex its tiny muscles and came down the web to gather and eat his evening meal. As soon as he reached his supper, things changed rapidly. The wasp spun in the web, turned upside down, and wrapped his legs around his would-be conqueror and held tight. Then he somehow broke the web and flew away with the little spider, and the last time I saw the spider, his victory was turned into defeat, the victim became the victor, and the victor became the victim.

Remember how the Rose of Sharon was put under the sentence of the cross and death with its skeleton hand clutched ever so tightly to His throat? Those watching thought, "Surely He will come down." But He didn't. There He hung, a withered rose, a broken stem, a crushed petal, almost unrecognizable as a man. The fragrance of a life that once sweetened the air was reduced to the stench of blood and sweat. The earth quaked in horror as the lightning flashed out of the midday midnight sky. The birds hushed their singing and the children quit playing. We hear the thunder crash like the booming of a thousand cannons on the field of battle. We see the rain fall and wash His blood-soaked, matted hair where they had pierced His brow with a crown of thorns. He cried out the first time in a manger thirty-three years before and broke the silence of a stable; now He cries out in agony on a cross for the last time, "It is finished," and He died.

There was that frozen moment in time when God was dead. Never again would an infant cheek be flushed with rosy redness. Never again would a flower smell sweet. Never again would the rain wash away the dew of the morning. Never again would a robin sing its fresh song in the dawn. Never again would joy be in the earth or laughter in the human heart, for God was dead.

The Roman centurion screamed out the order to take his lifeless body down. Joseph of Arimathaea, after secretly arranging for His broken, riveted body, wrapped it in grave clothes and had it brought to a new sepulcher for proper burial. Christ's own disciples turned away and hid, locked in their prison of fear and disappointment, never to believe again. Every dream, hope, and ambition that they ever conceived was abbreviated and compressed to the height, depth and width of that tomb. These disciples were engulfed in a sea of hopelessness for the best they had ever known in life and the highest they had ever seen was buried in the tomb. It was over for hope was shattered and the Rose was dead. But that was Friday! Sunday's coming. Friday's victim became Sunday's victor and the devil became the victim!

In the city of Atlanta a wealthy banker, while walking on the street, was attracted to a portrait that hung in the window of an art gallery. The artist had graphically portrayed the dying Christ that cruel, dismal day at Calvary. The banker was mesmerized and brought under the stirring whisper of the colored canvas. He was held in suspended animation. Suddenly there came a jolt to his coattail. He turned and saw a little shoeshine boy, not much older than ten. With tears in his eyes he said, "Mister, they took my Jesus, and they killed my Jesus, and Mister, my Jesus died." Then he picked up his shoeshine gear and quietly walked away. The man immediately turned back for there was something hypnotic about that portrait. After a few minutes passed, suddenly, like a bolt of electricity, the shoeshine boy was running back, dropped his gear, grabbed the man around the waist and said with jubilation, "Mister, I said they took my Jesus and they killed my Jesus and my Jesus died. But, Mister, there is something I forgot to tell you, my Jesus didn't stay dead!"

On the third day the Rose of Sharon bloomed again! Hell was the first to know because early Sunday morning a light appeared at the end of the darkness. The Son of God lifted the gates of eternal damnation off their rusty hinges, threw them aside, and waded through the ashes and burning coals of the empire of the doomed and the damned. Coming to the devil's palace, He kicked the door in, grabbed Satan by the neck and cast him off his imperial throne. Then he snatched the keys from Satan's tight grip, put one foot on the devil and one foot on the crumbling empire of death, and, in a flash, He raised His hands to the Father and said to you and me, "I am alpha and omega, the first and the last, and what you call the end I call the beginning!" Your life is not futile; your sickness is not fatal because His death was not final. Up from the grave he arose. The Rose of Sharon bloomed again!

Chapter
3

Life's Unanswered Questions

*And at the ninth hour Jesus cried with a loud
voice, saying, Eloi, Eloi, lama sabachthani?
which is, being interpreted, My God, my God,
why hast thou forsaken me?*

Mark 15:34

On an October day in 1999 I stood on the side of a little
Missouri hill. As far as cemeteries go, it was the most
serene I have ever seen. My purpose was not to enjoy the
changing leaves of fall or to admire the beauty of this unique
little graveyard, but to bury a friend, and not just a friend, but
a mentor, a teacher, an example, and most of all, a man of
God. There was irony as the casket was lowered. For the casket that was filling the hole in the earth was the same casket

that was creating the hole in my heart. I poised myself in a most dignified manner, but my emotions were crushed and wrung out. I had one question that to this day is absent of an answer: Why was Robert Holmes, the greatest missionary I have ever known, having done more for God than most men could do in two lifetimes, struck down in the prime of life at the age of forty-eight? Suddenly, without announcement God took him. I have to be honest; it just doesn't make sense. Life itself is sometimes a mystery. We've been fed a lie that being a Christian exempts us from tragedy, sickness, and pain. Faith can do a lot of things, but it's not a magic charm that wards off every bad situation. Life is full of problems that have no answers.

At times life just doesn't make sense. It doesn't make sense when you stand in the funeral home looking at the child God gave you, the same child you dedicated to Him who just the day before was full of energy but now is cold and lifeless. It doesn't make any sense when your spouse of ten, fifteen, twenty, or twenty-five years tells you, "I don't love you anymore, but I've found someone I do." It doesn't make sense when the doctor says your condition is incurable, terminal, when you've been faithful to God and lived and stood on His word. It just doesn't make any sense. Oh, I know there are these super-powered faith preachers who never get sick, have a sore throat, headache, flat tire, ingrown toenail, or postnasal drip. They tell us there is a realm of faith we can live in that we can live above tragedy, sickness, or the bad things of life. I'm sorry I do not swallow that illusionary Alice in Wonderland doctrine, because I live in another realm; it's called the realm of reality.

Sickness is real. Disappointment is real. Pain and grief are real. Broken dreams, open-heart surgery, cancer and divorce are all real. My faith is not always going to keep me from it, but my faith is always going to keep me through it! My faith doesn't always keep me from the fiery furnace, but it will keep me while I am in it and carry me through.

A few days ago my family and I took a tour through the Bombing Memorial and Museum in Oklahoma City, Oklahoma. Being a native of that great city, I have an added sense of betrayal and sadness in my heart. Though Oklahoma City is large, in essence those were my people, in my hometown. Maneuvering from one phase to the other, experiencing the realism of this true life tragedy of human drama, I was moved to tears. The memorial was a reminder of the dastardly devised execution of one hundred sixty-eight living, loving mortal people, red-blooded people just like my children, my wife, my brother, my sister, my mom or my dad. Why? God only knows. While we were reading the names of the victims, I made a remarkable discovery that had been unknown to me for years. A woman with the unusual last name of Koelsch appeared on the list. It's a German name, my mother's maiden name. I called my mother and asked if she was aware that one of the victims shared her last name. "Well, of course," she replied. "She was one of my distant cousins." I never knew until that day how close to home the Oklahoma City bombing really came. It just doesn't make any sense.

We read in Hebrews 11 what we often call Faith's Hall of Fame. We read of Abraham, Abel, Noah, Moses, and others who through faith "subdued kingdoms, quenched the violence of fire, escaped the edge of the sword, out of weakness were made strong, waxed valiant in fight, turned to flight the armies of the aliens. Women received their dead raised to life again." This, no doubt, is a testimony of faith. Faith can move mountains and bring healing and deliverance. But, this is only one dimension of faith. Faith is three dimensional so you must read on to get the whole picture:

> *"And others were tortured, not accepting deliverance; that they might obtain a better resurrection: While others had trial of cruel mockings and scourgings, yea, moreover of bonds and imprisonment: They were stoned, they were sawn asunder, were destitute, afflicted, tormented; (Of whom the world was not worthy :) they wandered in deserts, and in mountains, and in dens and caves of the earth."*

Paul, the man who penned Hebrews 11 and who said by faith some escaped the edge of the sword, didn't escape himself. He was decapitated by a razor-sharp Roman sword. His faith didn't get him out of it, but his faith got him through it. His testimony is recorded in 2 Timothy 4:6. (Paraphrased)

> *"For I am now ready to be offered, and the time of my departure is athand. I have fought a good fight, I have finished my course, I have kept the faith: Hell has tried to knock it out of me but I have kept it! I have been cast down, persecuted, troubled on every side, shipwrecked, stoned, the*

gale force winds have blown against me and there were times life hasn't made a bit of sense but I have kept the faith and by God's grace I am going to hold on till the end. Henceforth there is laid up for me a crown of righteousness, which the Lord, the righteous judge, shall give me at that day: and not to me only, but unto all them also that love his appearing."

Paul wrote to the Corinthian church in his second letter that at times we are "perplexed." The word perplexed in the Greek is "aporeo", pronounced "ap-or-eh'-o, and means to be at a loss mentally, bewildered or to be puzzled. Just because we as Christians have the Answer (Jesus Christ) doesn't necessarily mean we have all the answers to all of life's questions. We are not always going to be whistling in the sunshine. It rains on the just and the unjust, and, when it rains, it pours; and, when it pours, it gets dark. It's a dark time when you are sick in your body. It's a dark time when you're in financial struggle. You're staying up all night adding up the numbers, and they still won't add. You know one hundred or even fifty dollars would make all the difference in the world, but it's just not there. A thousand dollars could turn your life around. It's a dark time when relationships that have value and meaning are damaged and destroyed beyond repair. It's a dark time when death comes and snatches a loved one, and hopelessness and despair invade your heart. It can become so intense you'll even wonder if there is a God, and, if there is, He is obviously not interested in you. I don't care how saved you are, how sanctified you are, how anointed you are, darkness can come around you till you'll cry out, "My God, my God, why has thou forsaken me?"

People have wrestled with the "whys" of life from the very beginning. There are just some things in life that were never meant for us to know. Jesus said to His disciples in the book of Acts 1:7, "It is not for you to know." Little Billy couldn't understand why the Lord put so many vitamins in green beans instead of chocolate candy. In the first miracle of changing the water into wine Jesus demonstrated that everything He does doesn't always make sense. They needed wine not water. But, Jesus told them to fill the six water pots with water as to say, "This may not have any logic, but trust me." You may not know what He is doing, but in all things trust Him nevertheless. This is the whole point of faith. It believes in spite of what it sees. We walk by faith and not by sight.

There are things in life that happen to us all, and in those times it is imperative to our survival that we feel with our heart instead of think with our head. Ezekiel the prophet puts everything in perspective when asked by God if those dry bones can live again. "And I answered, O LORD GOD, THOU KNOWEST," (Ezekiel 37:3). Ezekiel was saying, "Lord, I can't say yes, and I can't say no because I'm looking at these dry bones and they are real. I know the difference between.

Life and death
   Victory and defeat
      Health and sickness
         Going over and going under.

To be honest I'm just really not sure, but I also know that you are God and have all power. You can speak a word, and dead men shall live, O Lord God, Thou knowest! God you know everything. You know my down sitting and my up rising. You know my labor and my leisure. You never slumber nor sleep, Thou knowest."

There were times I didn't understand, and life just didn't make any sense. I didn't know what to do or where to go. Every door seemed shut and it appeared as though things would never come around. My family didn't understand me, and my friends couldn't help me. In those times I had to say, "God you know. You know all about me; the hairs of my head are numbered. You guard my bed at night and order my steps in the day." So why should I be discouraged and why should the shadows fall? Why should I feel so lonely and long for heaven and home? Why, when Jesus is my portion, my constant friend is He. Why, when His eye is on the sparrow, and I know He watches me.

Life doesn't always make sense now, but that doesn't mean it will never make sense. All things work together for our good. For many years, no doubt, the Old Testament Joseph couldn't put the pieces of the puzzle together. But one day it all fit, and the eyes of his understanding were opened. What his brothers meant for his bad, God meant for his good. Psalms 119:67-68 says, "Before I was afflicted I went astray: but now I have kept thy word. Thou art good and doest good." The seventy-first verse of the same chapter records, "It was good for me that I have been afflicted; that I might learn thy statutes." We have been programmed to think that all afflictions are bad. I admit that none of us, including myself, wants trouble, but at times we need it, and it is for our good.

On a very blustery afternoon a man threw his suitcase and other bags in the back of his car and raced off to the airport to catch a scheduled flight. On the way he developed a painful stomach ache that almost rendered him helpless. He knew there was no way he could go through the hassle of getting a parking place, checking in his bag, finding the terminal and boarding the airplane; he was too sick. Regretfully, he turned his car around and sped back to his home. Upon arrival he hurriedly ran up the stairs and into the bathroom. After getting sick he fell into his bed strategically placing a trash can beside him. As he was lamenting his illness and missed business opportunity, he turned the television on. A news brief flashed on the screen. The same airplane that he was scheduled to be on had crashed after take-off, killing everyone on board. It doesn't take the wisdom of King Solomon to understand the man's sickness was good for him.

Speaking of the Wisdom of Solomon, Proverbs 3:5-6 tell us, "Trust in the LORD with all thine heart; and lean not unto thine own understanding. In all thy ways acknowledge him, and he shall direct thy paths." Everything in our life may not be good, but everything in the life of a believer eventually works out for his or her good.

A few decades ago a young boy was in a car wreck. His left leg was severed from his body leaving him on the edge of life. He recovered but was left with a wooden leg from just below his hip. As he would stand watching the other boys run and play games, bitterness developed in his soul because he could not. He had one burning question that seemed to haunt him day and night, "Why?" He went through life with a peg leg and a heart full of bitterness. "Why God did you let this happen to me?" It just didn't make any sense and sure wasn't fair. One night after he had grown older (somewhere in his late twenties) he received an invitation from a friend to attend a revival meeting, so he went. At the altar call he felt compelled to come to Christ, so to the altar he came. He prayed through and left his sins and all his bitterness at the cross. The Lord saved him and called him to the mission field. After four years of missions training he left for the continent of Africa. Soon after his arrival he was captured by a tribe of cannibals. But before they could eat him he quietly snatched a knife from one of the tribesmen and in the presence of the king he sliced off a piece of his leg (his peg leg) and handed it to the monarch. The king bit down upon the wood and instantly spit it out and said in his native tongue "no good, no good." The king spared the missionary's life. He said he never questioned God again, and the scripture Romans 8:28 was solidified forever in his heart: "And we know that all things work together for good to them that love God, to them who are the called according to his purpose."

What do you do when, like the wise men, you follow a star thinking something grand and glorious is just over the hill and in the next city, but, instead, your diligent and ever-extensive journey brings you to a barn full of livestock? What do you do when you follow a star and find a stable? Instead of a magnificent golden palace with a king all garbed in royal apparel sitting on an ivory throne with a pearl scepter in his powerful hand, you find a poor young Jewish mother in a horse barn with a little baby held tight within her arms? This is nothing that you anticipated or expected. Can you imagine the disappointment of the three wise men when their journey finally ended in Bethlehem? Have you ever followed a star and found a stable? When you started it seemed so promising. The future seemed as unlimited as the stars of the night, but something unexpected happened and all your dreams were reduced to the dimensions of a stable.

Perhaps out of the blue your soul mate, your spouse, the mother or the father of your precious children for reasons beyond your control terminates a life-long commitment, and the happy years you spent together have been thrown to the lions of betrayal. It seemed so promising that distant day so long ago as you both stood before the marriage altar, but now it is forever over. Or maybe it's the long-awaited promotion. Your employer tells you have been passed over. You walk out of his office dejected, realizing you've been following a star but you've ended your search in a stable. I have seen people save all their working lives for the golden day of retirement, and right when it was within their grasp, they became ill and had to spend their life savings to stay alive, and the quality of life is abridged to nursing aid in some forgotten home for the sick and elderly. The scenarios are endless, as well as the questions.

As pastor, I hear success from books and conference speakers, and, yes, it has its place. No doubt we all love success because it feels good to succeed. But life is not one big utopia. As a matter of fact, most of life is trial and error, and lots of error. Let me offer just a little insight in the life of the three wise men. God had a purpose, though at the time they could not see it, and as an example, if you will dare to follow them, you will be also wise indeed.

1. Wise men look for Christ when they find a stable
2. Wise men still offer their best to Christ even though the stable is not what they were expecting
3. Wise men allow the stable to change their course in life "They departed into their own country another way."

(Matthew 2:12)

God has a bigger plan than yours and if in this life you never get an answer, I can make this promise: if you will just trust the Lord with all your heart, you will understand it better by and by. Questions will be turned into answers. Tragedy will be transformed into triumph. Pain will be lost in paradise. "Weeping may endure for the night but joy cometh in the morning," (Psalms 30:5). "O Lord God, Thou knowest." Isn't it good to know, when you don't know and life doesn't make sense, God knows, so trust Him.

Chapter 4

When Fear Knocks

*Thou shalt tread upon the lion and adder: the young lion
and the dragon shalt thou trample under feet.*

Psalms 91:13

While in the safety and comfort of her own little home, Emma, who had just turned eighty-two her last birthday, was sitting and talking with the Lord. Suddenly, there came a knock on the door. She looked out the peephole and saw Fear standing on her front porch. She immediately went back and sat down without opening the door. Then she turned, looked at the Lord and said, "Jesus, there is someone at the door for you."

There is only one way to deal with fear, and that is with faith; faith in Jesus Christ! The Lord told John on the Isle of Patmos "Fear not; I am the first and the last," (Rev. 1:17). In other words, Jesus was saying, "John, don't be afraid. I was here before there was anything to fear, and I will be here long after everything you fear is gone." Fear is a thief that steals and strips you of everything you hold dear. What has fear stolen from you? Peace of mind or confidence of a better life? Fear destroys sound sleep and contributes to heart attacks, high blood pressure, and nervous disorders. The Bible is clear; fear is simply a lack of faith in God; Faith in the purpose and promise of Almighty God. In 2 Timothy 1:7, we read "For God hath not given us the spirit of fear; but of power, and of love, and of a sound mind."

Fear is a very common emotion and we find its genesis in the first book of the Bible. After the fall of Adam the first reaction of being a sinner was fear. Adam said to God "We were afraid so we went and hid ourselves." The fears that paralyze are too numerous to list. They range from fear of life to fear of death, and include fear of failure, fear of success, fear of sickness, fear of old age, fear of dying young, fear of rejection, fear of poverty, fear of staying, fear of leaving. This is a fact: Where disease has killed thousands, fear has killed tens of thousands. Register your fears over the span of twenty years and you will realize most of the things we fear never happen to us. The prophet Elijah ran for his life in fear of Queen Jezebel. She sent the word that she was going to kill him, so he thought with his feet instead of his head, and he ran and kept running. But the thing he feared never happened. As a matter of fact, not only did the prophet not die at the hands of the wicked queen, but Elijah never died, period! The thing you fear will probably never happen either.

Alexander the Great rode a beautiful black warhorse, Bucephalus. Horse traders brought the horse to the court of King Phillip, Alexander's father, in hopes that he would buy it for his cavalry. The horse proved too wild in its nature; no one could tame it let alone ride it. It was rejected by the king's horsemen, but Alexander was greatly taken with the beauty of the beast and privately petitioned his father to allow him to personally train the animal. King Phillip gave his sanction and Alexander went to work. He had noticed and been keenly attentive to the problem that no one else had discovered. The horse was afraid of his own shadow. Alexander turned the horse into the sun and trained him accordingly until this mighty horse was able to conquer its fear. The things that most people fear are usually just shadows; there is no substance. Why don't you turn into the sun and cast the shadow behind you? "For the Lord God is a sun" (Psalm 84:11). David said in Psalm 23, "He leadeth me in the paths of righteousness for His name's sake. Yea, though I walk through the valley of the shadow of death, I will fear no evil: for thou *art* with me." As the Shepherd led, the shadow of the valley was cast behind him and David looked continually into the sun. Why did Peter sink down into the water that fearful night? He quit walking into the sun.

The Bible has a lot to say about fear and the victory over it. When Christ was born at Bethlehem the angels told the shepherds who watched their flocks by night, "Fear not because today the Christ is born in the city of David." Jesus said, "Fear not, be not afraid, let not your heart be troubled, have faith in God."

Late one night while coming through the mountains of New Mexico making my way up the steep and winding road I suddenly noticed a sign that had been posted by the highway department that read, "Watch for falling rocks." At that juncture in life there were only three in our family, my wife, my oldest son and me; however, that night we picked up an unwelcome hitchhiker: Fear. Fear took over, and though I was at the wheel, it was very evident fear was in control as he smoothly whispered, "What if?" What if one of those huge boulders that were ever as big or bigger than our vehicle came rolling down the mountainside? It would surely be sudden death for all of us. As I hugged the side of the mountain, looking up and trying to penetrate the darkness, white knuckles on the steering wheel, my imagination fueled by fear was running wild. After several miles of prayer and torment, I had enough and felt it was time to put my unwanted, uninvited, and undesirable backseat driver out. I had come to the conclusion that there was absolutely nothing I could do to stop falling rocks. If it were meant to be, it would be. If the rocks were going to fall, they would fall. I could not continue the drive under such strain. Three choices were before me:

1. Turn around, go back, and live the rest of my life on that side of the mountain
2. Drive on and worry the rest of the journey
3. Drive on to my destination; trust God and be free of fear

I chose the third, and lived happily ever after. What good has worry ever done for me? It wouldn't hold the rock up there, nor would it jar it loose. The bottom line is: Fear didn't even remotely impinge on or affect the rocks, but it had a monstrous affect upon me. Life is full of signs that give warning, "Watch for falling rocks." You can quit; be miserable the rest of life's trip or you can go on and trust God Who, by the way, created the rock to begin with.

A six-year old boy called out in the night and told his mother he was afraid of the dark. His mother reassured him there was nothing to be afraid of because Jesus was with him. He replied, "Mom, I know Jesus is with me but I want something with some skin on it." We laugh, but we can be just as guilty. The promises of God are real to every believer; however, when fear knocks on our door, we have the tendency to disregard His promises and want something a little more tangible. Here is something you can hold on to: Read Psalms 91 and you will find a fresh courage to overcome fear, worry, and anxiety. In verse 13 of this chapter God's Word gives us the three classifications of fear and what to do. "Thou shalt tread upon the lion and adder: the young lion and the dragon shalt thou trample under feet."

1. The Lion & Young Lion: Undisguised Fear.

The lion is the king of all beasts, and he roars through the jungle. He announces his presence to every creature as if to say, "I'm here, and you'd better get out of my way!" The zebra loses his stripes. The hippopotamus goes under water while the monkeys climb to the highest branch because of fear. Life has its undisguised fears. They are real, and they make their presence known. Our nation is plagued by crime. The schoolhouse has become a slaughter house. Violence, gangs, terrorism and drugs are all factual and undisguised.

In a dense corner of the jungle a large male lion came roaring through. He roared up to the python and said, "Who is the king of the jungle around here?" The terrified snake said, "You are your majesty." The lion said, "That's right and don't you forget it." Then he roared up to the gazelle and said in a very intimidating tone, "Who is the king of the jungle around here?" The gazelle screamed out with fear, "Please don't eat me, sir; you are, O Great One. Long live the King!" Again the lion said, "That's right and don't you forget it!" The lion then came up to a big bull elephant and roared and repeated his sixty-four million dollar question, "Who is the king of the jungle around here?" The elephant looked down with a very annoying look on his face. Then he wrapped his trunk around the want-to-be king and began to beat him against the rocks until the old lion was almost unconscious. Then, he took him and just pitched him up into the top of a tree. The lion beat, bruised, and bloody look down as the big bull elephant was lumbering off and said, "Okay, buddy, you didn't have to get mad just because you didn't know the answer." Well, I know the answer, and it's not the devil nor is it fear. Jesus Christ is the King of all Kings and the Lord of all Lords. Sure, there are real life fears that you and I have no control over. The newspapers are full of them. The news doesn't really change from week to week and even year to year. The faces and the names change, but the stories remain the same: Rape, disaster, murder, and mayhem. These are real fears that don't parade incognito. Fear, much like a lion, has no mercy. So, have no mercy on undisguised fear. Put it where it belongs— under your feet through the power of Jesus Christ.

2. The Adder: Unexpected Fear.

A snake is an unexpected creature that usually shows up in the most unexpected places. You are taking a leisurely walk down your favorite trail, and, as you step over a log, there it is, unexpected; and, no matter what your religious upbringing is, you will do a Pentecostal jig. If you don't believe in dancing, you will dance. I went fishing one day with three brothers. Ronnie, Jerry and Simon Young. We weren't very successful casting our artificial lures and worms. Either it just wasn't a good day, or we just weren't very convincing to the fish. In the evaluation of our fruitless efforts I decided we were fishing on the wrong side of the pond. So I picked up my pole and fishing tackle and began to walk the other side. As I was crossing the dam of the pond, I turned and looked down at the bottom and saw a snake haphazardly sleeping on the fence undoubtedly enjoying the warmth of the sun. I yelled back to my friends, "Hey, there is a snake over here, and I am going to kill him." Then, I looked for the biggest stick I could find, and after finding it I proceeded very cautiously down the side of the dam stalking my poisonous prey. Half way down the dam, I discovered an electric fence. Not knowing whether or not it was on, I sure wasn't going to touch it to find out. So, I just stepped over it and kept creeping with stealth-like motions. Finally, after reaching my sleeping, slithering foe

I pulled back the stick and with a force equal to Mark McGuire hitting a five hundred fifty foot home run I struck that snake with full force right between the eyes. To my amazement it only disoriented him and did not knock him completely out. Like molasses being poured out, the snake instinctively started sliding off the fence toward the water. There was no way I was going to let the snake get away that easily, so I stuck my stick under his belly and balanced it in the middle of his body and started to back up the hill. In my mind I imagined the snake suddenly snapping out of his bewilderment, leaping off the stick, and striking me with his poisonous fangs before I had a chance to back up the hill and finish the job. All of a sudden I backed into that electric fence, and it was on! I screamed like a stuck hog. My friends jumped up and with emotion yelled, "Did he get you?" I yelled back, "No, but this electric fence did!"

Unexpected fear—it may come as a knock on the door or a phone call or at the doctor's office after a routine checkup. You may start your day in the sunshine, and before the day is over abruptly you might find yourself in a storm. Suddenly out of nowhere fear sinks its fangs into you and releases enough venom to paralyze a grown man. Never forget at that point in your life God gives you power to tread upon unexpected fear.

3. The Dragon: Unfounded Fear.

Have you ever seen a dragon? They are huge, and they breathe fire and crush cities. But are you afraid of a dragon? No, they are only fictional; they really don't exist. We make mountains out of molehills and see a devil behind every door. We are afraid of things that will never happen. You think you are going to go broke with nothing to verify that. You're afraid your son will never get married, and he is only three years old. You are constantly thinking that you are going to die with something that only one out of every three billion people dies of.

Most of our worries are borrowed from another day. We worry about mountains we will never have to climb and rivers we will never have to cross. The two women who came to anoint the body of Jesus after the crucifixion missed so much because of unfounded fear. It was a glorious time that first resurrection morning. The air was crisp with the smell of spring in every breeze. Radiant wildflowers with every color of the rainbow were in full bloom along the roadside. The sun was rising in its majestic splendor, sparkling upon the snow-capped peaks of the mighty mountains. A mystique electrified the atmosphere, yet they missed it all. Why? Because all they could worry about was, "Who is going to roll away the stone to let us in?" Once they arrived they discovered their fear was in vain. The stone was already rolled away, and the angel of the Lord was sitting on top of it. He asked the two women this penetrating question, "Why seek ye the living among the dead? He is not here but He is risen, come see where He laid!"

I dreamed one night that I was in a great convention hall at a pastor's conference. As I was intently listening to the speaker, out of nowhere, three, small, five-foot tall elephants entered the meeting. One of them was for some rea-

son attracted to me. I was trying to ignore it, hoping it
would just go away, but it didn't. The elephant took its tail,
wrapped it around my leg and jerked me out of my chair.
Then, without warning, it dragged me down the aisle, out
the door and up the street. The whole time I was kicking
and screaming for it to stop, but it didn't. At this point I
only had one weapon left. I started shouting, "I rebuke you
in the name of Jesus," over and over again. Each time the
hold was loosened until it finally lost hold. Then I immediately leaped to my feet and ran as fast as I could back to the
convention hall. Just as I was entering the door, I turned and
to my horror the little elephant was running back to get me.
Once inside the building I made an amazing discovery. The
convention hall had been converted into a restaurant, and all
the preachers were now eating. I cased the room quickly,
knowing time was of the essence. Against the wall was a
table that spanned twenty feet. In my reasoning I thought,
if I could get behind the table and crawl to the end, the elephant would never find me. So, I quickly fell to the ground
and on my hands and knees crawled to the end until my
head was butted up against the wall. I felt safe. Then, suddenly, to my shock, the little elephant found me and with its
trunk it began to caress my hair. I can't describe the fear
that struck my heart; so much that I immediately woke, to
find my sleeping wife caressing the top of my head.
Unfounded fear! The devil wants to invade and dominate
your mind with any and every fictional scenario he can
come up with. Don't let it happen to you. Don't allow yourself to go on an emotional roller-coaster ride. Kick
unfounded fear in the seat of the britches and put it under

your feet with the Word of God.

Several years ago one of my greatest fears was the fear of flying. From the first time I boarded an airplane, I was afraid. I remarked to the man sitting beside me, "Look at those cars; they look like ants." The man replied, "They are ants, son, we haven't taken off yet." Yet, in all seriousness, for years flying in the wild blue yonder was one of my greatest nightmares. On a flight from Memphis, Tennessee, to Houston, Texas, our plane flew into a storm. I had in the course of ministry flown many times, and without exception I was afraid every time. This was the first time I had ever been in a storm at thirty-five thousand feet above the earth. Needless to say, I thought I was going to die as that plane rocked, dropped, and bounced all over that sky. I started praying what I believed to be my last prayer. Then I noticed him: Two seats in front of me on the other aisle was an airline captain. He had flown all his flights and was now heading home to Houston. I noticed something else: He was never frightened or afraid as he calmly read his evening paper. Here is the conclusion I came to: That captain had no doubt spent thousands of hours in the air in the course of his career. He knew what to expect and what to fear. So for the next hour or so I never took my eyes off him. If he wasn't afraid, I wasn't afraid. If he was calm, I was calm. Now, if he had jumped up with wide eyes and ran to the cockpit, pushing the attendants out of the way, they would have buried me on that plane because I would have died with a heart attack. In life you will have storms, and fear will try to crowd in on you from every side. But here is the secret: Jesus Christ is the Captain of salvation. Keep Your Eyes On

The Captain! He's already been there and done that, and He's not afraid so you don't have to be either. When fear knocks on your door, let faith answer, "Jesus, there is someone at the door for you."

Chapter
5

The Tenacity of Bulldog Faith

But he answered and said, it is not meet to take the children's bread, and cast it to dogs. And she said, Truth, Lord: yet the dogs eat of the crumbs which fall from their masters' table. Then Jesus answered and said unto her, O woman, great is thy faith: be it unto thee even as thou wilt. And her daughter was made whole from that very hour.

Matthew 15:26-28

*O*ne clear, sunny day a businessman observed a small boy in a vacant field pulling against what seemed an impossible task. The boy had both hands around a pesky weed trying with all his might to uproot it. With sweat on his brow and determination in his heart the little fellow would not let go. After a while suddenly the weed gave up; the root let go causing the boy to fly back, crashing safely on his padded backside. The man remarked, "You sure had a hard time getting that weed to come up, didn't you, son?" The boy replied, "I sure did, sir. THE WHOLE WORLD WAS AGAINST ME!" Do you ever feel like the whole world is against you? Sure you do. Right now, even as you read this book, you may feel your life is unraveling, and you are left with only one question, "What can I do?" I believe the answer is found in the pages of the living Word of God!

In Matthew, the story of the Syrophenician woman, cited above, we are entrusted with an example of bulldog faith and the power of tenacity. The word "tenacity" means "stubborn persistency, holding fast, cohesive, sticking, and adhesive." Like super glue it is the banding of two articles together making them next to impossible to separate. This is the kind of faith God honors. It is tenacity like Jacob's. It was tenacity that caused Jacob to cry out to God, "I won't let you go until you bless me!"

The bulldog was bred by the British for the medieval sport of baiting bulls. Bulls are symbols of brutal strength. They can whirl, turn, stomp, gore, and move with unbelievable agility. There is nothing more terrifying and dangerous than a two thousand pound, enraged bull. In the ancient sport of bull baiting, the bull's nose would be blown full of pepper to infuriate it to the maximum effect. Then into the arena came this little fifty-pound giant of a bulldog with bowed legs, broad chest, and the look of a champion. He was there for one reason: to win. He would grab the bull and with incredible tenacity hold on in spite of personal pain, weariness, against almost impossible odds. For hours they were in the throes of battle until the bull was worn down like a wounded deer, collapsing in total exhaustion. Then the jaws of the bulldog were pried off its defeated foe.

The faith that we possess is that tough. It has the tenacity to hold on; after it is hit, gored, knocked down, tried and tested, it holds on. When you are pushed and shoved, knocked back and forth and the foundations of the earth are crumbling all around you like sand castles on a beach, I want to remind you the Anchor still holds. Bulldog faith won't let go. An old man of God was asked to define persistent faith, and he replied, "First, you got to take hold. Second, you got to hold on, and, third, you got to never let go!"

Nature is full of the expression and example of tenacity. Only by restraint is life possible; look at the unseen power of gravity, the germination of a seed, or the faithful beating of a human heart. Who hasn't seen a soft mushroom lift heavy masses of hard pavement through expansion, or a tender root split a rock by its growth? Walk out to a country pond on a hot summer day and look past the reeds and cattails and you will see tenacity in action as air bubbles make their way to the surface. It's God's way of saying through nature, "You can't keep a good man down." That's why I love bubbling Christians, you just can't keep them down. They have that uncanny ability to rise up again in spite of whatever is pushing them down. Like the children sing:

"It's bubbling, it's bubbling, it's bubbling in my soul
I'm singing, I'm shouting since Jesus made me whole
Folks don't understand it and I cannot tell you why
But it's a bub, bub, bub
Bub, bub bub, bubbling day and night!"

Do I fully understand how that works? No, but neither do I understand how black cows can eat green grass and give white milk. Faith in Jesus Christ really does work.

I am personally a great lover of the ocean. I love the smell of salt water in the air. The sound of seagulls and the sight of a lighthouse have a stimulating effect upon me. There is a pull on me to gravitate to the coast like a sea turtle. Sitting on the beach and watching the tide roll in and out is therapy for my mind. The reason that the ocean tide rolls back away from the shore is to gather itself together, joining itself to the strength of more water to be thrust forward in another dynamic explosion upon the sandy beach. Much like the Syrophenician woman, you may feel as though you have been pushed back, and maybe the devil has said to you that you are all washed-up. You may be washed-up, but not in the sense that the enemy has whispered. You have been washed-out only to re-gather your strength to be washed up on the shore line of God's purpose, and to fulfill His destiny in you—so don't disregard your faith.

Throughout our nation's Civil War one of the most strategic positions held during a bloody battle was that of a flag-bearer, or better termed, the standard-bearer. On both sides the flags flapped in the breeze with pride, but it was not just a decoration, it was a proclamation. It stood to give direction while the cannons were exploding with thunderous sound and the smoke was thick as southern molasses, while the muskets spun out smoldering powder and lead like tomorrow would never come. When on either side the flag-bearer was shot down, the old bullet-ridden flag would fall to the ground, but it wouldn't stay there long. Another soldier would lay down his gun, pick up the banner, raise it high, and look the enemy in the eyes, and shout, "We've not given up yet!" There may be those around us who have been shot down, and in this final hour of warfare it seems that the standard has been lowered, but I am glad to tell you that God has an army. God's army is coming and grabbing that blood stained banner, holding it high, and shouting to the enemy, "We've not given up yet!" As a matter of fact, God told us in Isaiah 59:19, "So shall they fear the name of the Lord from the west, and his glory from the rising of the sun. When the enemy shall come in like a flood, the Spirit of the Lord shall lift up a standard against him."

In one church as the pastor so faithfully labored, he was met by small band of resistance. They let him know that they were there before he got there, and they would be there after he left. Being a constant thorn in his flesh, their guerilla tactics became more than he thought he could bear, so he set his heart to resign. First, he called his district superintendent and broke the news to him: "I can't take any more so I quit." The superintendent replied, "Son, can I ask you a few questions before you do? Have they ever spit in your face?" The young preacher said, "No, of course not." The superintendent asked,

"Well do they ever smite you in the face?" "No," was the reply. Again, the superintendent asked, "Have they ever stripped, scourged, and crucified you?" The young preacher answered, "No, and God being my helper until they do, I'll hold on."

What kind of faith do you have? Some people have fair weather faith. Just as long as there is not a spiritual cloud in their sky and as long as the mosquitoes are not biting and the fish are, they can be on top with a little bit of victory. However, let the bills pile up and the in-laws pile in. Let life get just a little complicated, and their faith collapses like a house of cards. I am not a rocket scientist, but I can tell you if you have a fair weather faith you will never make it. The good news is the Lord wants you to reach the goal. Jesus was thrilled with the Syrophenician woman's tenacity which was a testimony to her bulldog faith.

1. Bulldog Faith is VIOLENT IN ITS OUTCRY

Faith won't take "no" for an answer. Luke 18:1 says, "And he spake a parable unto them to this end, that men ought always to pray, and not to faint." Then, Jesus lays out for us a graphical story of an unjust judge and a widow, saying,

"There was in a city a judge, which feared not God, neither regarded man: And there was a widow in that city; and she came unto him, saying, Avenge me of mine adversary. And he would not for a while: but afterward he said within himself, Though I fear not God, nor regard man; Yet because this widow troubleth me, I will avenge her, lest by her continual coming she weary me. And the Lord said, Hear what

the unjust judge saith. And shall not God avenge his own elect, which cry day and night unto him, though he bear long with them? I tell you that he will avenge them speedily. Nevertheless when the Son of man cometh, shall he find faith on the earth?"

Had it not been for her fatherless and fast-starving children, she would have soon been laid out of sight and out of hearing in her husband's forgotten grave. It was her orphaned and hungry children that made her to get violent in her outcry, and she would not give up but continually came with only one impassioned request, "Avenge me of my adversary!"

It is with the same violent faith that the woman from Canaan came to Jesus. There is a tinge of blood in the original ink that is lost in the tame translation, because there was a gleam of blood in the woman's wild eye when she approached that traveling small band of itinerant preachers. Almost psychotic, like an enraged she-bear robbed of her whelps, she lunged out and cried, "Have mercy on me, O Lord, and set my daughter free."

Jesus came to Canaan to get away from the crowds. He and His disciples needed to rest from ministry. Their physical bodies were fatigued, and they needed a little vacation. It was imperative to their well being that they escaped the multitudes for a short season. People were always pulling on Jesus, always wanting something from Him. His fame was such in His native land that He told His disciples, "Let's go somewhere where no one knows us." That's why the disciples said, "Lord let's send this woman away. We came here to get some rest and to get away from this very thing that is happening here. Of all the spots in the world we chose this

one because we wanted to be secluded and away from anyone that knows who you are, Lord. She's already announced
you as the son of David."

I can picture Peter saying, "Before you can turn around
there will be more lepers and sick folk than you can shake a
stick at. I'm tired and I need some rest." I can see Jesus
sending Andrew and John over, the two most diplomatic to
talk to this woman. "Look, lady. Here is Jesus' card. He is
on vacation right now. However, we will be back in the
office two weeks from tomorrow so please give us a call."
Then the woman replies, "I don't know who you are but you
better get out of my way, because I need a miracle for my
daughter." She was a living and breathing illustration of
Matthew 11:12: "And from the days of John the Baptist until
now the kingdom of heaven suffereth violence and the violent take it by force."

Complacency is a deadly enemy to your spiritual
progress. If you have all you want in God you'll never reach
out for more. You are not going to get anywhere with Christ
if you are satisfied with where you are at. Just drifting along
with the tide, getting stirred up a little on Sunday then drifting back into status quo on Monday is not the answer, for the
contented soul is a stagnant soul. You must press your way
in because there is nothing going to force you into it. If your
prayer is going to penetrate through the spiritual forces that
hinder you then you must become violent in your praying.
When you are violent it means you are against something.
As much as my faith is for healing it must be against sickness. My faith must come against the devil, against disease,
against depression and discouragement. You have to be tired

of being sick, tired of being depressed and defeated. You must be convinced that the devil doesn't want to free but God wants you healed, filled and delivered. If you ever move into that realm of reception then you must recognize there is a real enemy bent on keeping you from the victory and get a made up mind that what ever it takes, what ever it costs, you're going to press your way into God, hold it up, press your claim and say to God, "I'm going to have it before I quit."

2. Bulldog Faith is
VISIONARY IN ITS OUTLOOK.

As Jesus and his disciples were strolling along, a woman jumped out of nowhere and cried, "Have mercy on me!" Jesus kept walking and ignored her. Most of us would have been through with Him right there. "Who does He think He is? He's not that big and important. He just ignored me." There is something within our nature that detests being ignored. Being ignored is the worst form of rejection. In essence it is saying you are not worth the time or the breath that it would take to give you a reply or even a reaction. Jesus said to the woman, "It's not right to take the children's bread and give it to the dogs." Newer translations soften the blow and say, "Little dogs," not the wild, undomesticated dogs of the street but little house dogs. As far as I am concerned, a dog is a dog. It makes no difference whether someone calls you a Chow, or, if they call you a Chihuahua, you still have been called something not of your species. If you weren't through with Jesus when He walked by and ignored you, after He called you a dog, you were done. "Sick baby or no sick baby, what kind of nerve does he have calling me a dog?" But not this woman; she had a visionary outlook. She didn't see things as they were but rather how they were going to be. She looked beyond the mountain and saw the miracle. She looked past the sickness and saw the Savior. "Jesus you have the power, and I need a crumb of it to heal my daughter!"

When the need is great, you can take a lot. If the need is not great, you will get discouraged easily and give up. When you are the one who needs a miracle, prayer suddenly takes on a whole new dimension. When it's no longer a, "Now I lay me down to sleep," situation, but it has moved over into the context of do or die, you can pray and keep on praying. Jesus said all things are possible to them that believe. You have to see it before you can believe it. I heard of a marine biologist who tried to taint and discredit the Word of God. He studied a particular species of whale and in his final analysis concluded that the story of the prophet Jonah being swallowed by a whale could not be true. The cavity in its throat was too small making it impossible for a man to be lodged for three days and three nights. His problem was he didn't read the book. Jonah 1:17 says, "Now the Lord had prepared a great fish to swallow up Jonah." When the Lord prepares a fish, He can fix one with a living room, dining room, kitchen, microwave oven, gas stove, and an electric deepfreeze. Our God is Lord! What you see is what you get. Your vision will be focused, and nothing will get in the way.

3. Bulldog Faith is
VICTORIOUS IN ITS OUTCOME.

Then Jesus answered, "Woman you have great faith! Your request is granted." Her daughter was healed that very hour. Let me remind you that delay is not denial. We have been conditioned to believe and expect everything right now. We have developed a microwave faith mentality or an instant credit card confession, but it doesn't always work that way. An old preacher once told me that God could pull me through a knot whole, if I could stand the pull. To that I said, "God help me get another grip." What if the Church would have given up on the ninth day before the day of Pentecost? The ninth day in the upper room might have been discouraging. There was no sound, no cloven tongues of fire, no rushing wind, and no miracle—just an ordinary day like any other. But, they were patient as they waited; and on the tenth day, suddenly, there came a sound from heaven as of a "rushing mighty wind and it filled the entire house where they were sitting. And there appeared unto them cloven tongues like as of fire, and it sat upon each of them. And they were all filled with the Holy Ghost, and began to speak with other tongues, as the Spirit gave them utterance." Look what the Church received, just simply because they waited.

A new convert was standing in the altar one morning praying when he asked the Lord in a loud voice, "God, give me a trainload of patience." One of the old seasoned saints slipped up to him and said, "Son, you don't realize what you are asking for. When you ask God for a trainload of patience He always sends you two trainloads of tribulation." To that he looked back up and cried, "Lord, a thimble will do!" Tribulation worketh patience, and we need patience to endure. "For ye have need of patience, that, after ye have done the will of God, ye might receive the promise," (Hebrews 10:36). If you will hold on long enough, your answer will come. It's like a basketball player that gets in a slump. If he has a natural shot his coach is not going to tell him not to take it. He is going to say, "Keep shooting the ball, sooner or later it will fall." If it is true on the court, then how much more true is it in life? Don't quit praying. Don't quit believing. Don't quit pressing. It will fall. You may not know how, and you may not know when. It may be in the darkest hour, and the whole world may be against you, but hold on, **IT WILL FALL!**

Chapter
6

Jaith at the
Midnight Hour

And at midnight Paul and Silas prayed, and sang
praises unto God: and the prisoners heard them.

Acts 16:25

On a long open stretch of highway in West Texas, two Catholic nuns ran out of gas. An old farmer came along and offered to help, but realized he had nothing to put gas in, so he asked the two sisters if they had a container. They replied, "Yes, we both work at St. Michael's hospital, and we just happen to have a bed pan." After returning from many miles to get the gas, they stood there putting it in. A preacher came driving by and saw them putting the gas in using the bed pan and remarked; "Now that is real faith!" This is a humorous story that illustrates a pointed fact. Everyone has their definition and dogma of what real faith really is, even to the place that real faith has been abused and misused. For some faith is only a creative force that is always equated with materialism. It's what it can get for you, from cars to cash to condominiums. It is being taught that faith is like money—the more you have, the more you can buy, and the more you buy, the happier it will make you. But, that is just not true. Real faith is more than a debit card. It's more than a magic lamp that you rub when your deposits get a little lean. Real faith is enduring the pain and still serving God.

Faith is the God-given ability to keep believing His promises when His promises seem unbelievable. The emphasis is on God's ability because it's not our faith, it is His. Isaiah 59:19 states: "So shall they fear the name of the Lord from the west, and his glory from the rising of the sun. When the enemy shall come in like a flood, the Spirit of the Lord shall lift up a standard against him." We have all seen the devastating and destructive force of a flood. Once it reaches such violent proportions there is absolutely nothing that can be done to prevent it or slow it down. We have the technological know-how to fly to the far-flung regions of outer space, but we can't stop a flood after it reaches a certain stage. The enemy of your soul comes in like a flood with the same motive, to kill, steal, and to destroy. In that moment, when your faith runs dry, His faith is a sufficient supply.

Paul and Silas were stripped, beaten, and placed in the inner prison. Their feet were locked into stocks. Their legs were drawn far apart to slowly pull them out of joint. It was a pain-inflicting torture. The torment was even more intolerable because of the previous scourging. When the light of their faith grew dangerously low, at the last flicker of their flame of faith, the Spirit of the Lord relit their fire, and at midnight in the darkest hour they prayed and sang praises unto God. When the enemy came in like a flood, the Spirit of the Lord raised up a standard against him. When Paul and Silas should have been griping and complaining, they were praying and praising. Paul prayed when the sun shined and when the thunder rolled; he prayed in the palace and he prayed in the prison. He shares his secret with us in Ephesians 3:11-20:

> *"According to the eternal purpose which He purposed in Christ Jesus our Lord: In whom we have boldness and access with confidence by the faith of Him. Wherefore I desire that ye faint not at my tribulations for you, which is your glory. For this cause I bow my knees unto the Father of our Lord Jesus Christ, of whom the whole family in heaven and earth is named, that He would grant you, according to the riches of His glory, to be strengthened with might by His Spirit in the inner man; That Christ may dwell in your hearts by faith; that ye, being rooted and grounded in love, may be able to comprehend with all saints what [is] the breadth, and length, and depth, and height*

and to know the love of Christ, which passeth knowledge, that ye might be filled with all the full-ness of God. Now unto Him that is able to do exceeding abundantly above all that we ask or think, according to the power that worked in us."

God has made provision for every emergency of life. Within the human body God created an adrenal gland, that in times of danger and crisis, secretes large amounts of adrenalin through the bloodstream, giving you the power to do what is beyond your natural ability.

We have all read stories where mothers have picked up cars off their children or beaten back an attacker three times their size. When I was a boy my uncle, Rick Koelsch, who is four years older than I, had come to spend the night with my brother Tim and me. We were walking home that night when we approached a bridge about 100 yards away. Being a little mischievous, I came up with an irresistible plan of terror. I told him that the week prior; some boys were hacked up and mutilated by several murderers that were under the bridge. They were never caught so they were still there. Rick was older, but he was flatfooted, and in those days, a little over-weight and slow as a Christmas turkey. Tim and I were always able to outrun him. My plan was to get on the bridge, scream and take off running leaving my poor uncle in the dust, a frightened terrified, miserable human being. My brother was smart enough to figure out my plan, so he went right along with me. We drew closer and closer. The closer we got the more I built the suspense up. Rick just listened without saying much, and I knew I had another sucker on the hook. The bridge was dark without a light. The trees over-hung giving it an Alfred Hitchcock effect. As we stepped on the bridge, I screamed out, "There they are!" Then we took off, but, instead of our leaving him behind, he struck out at lightning speed and all we saw were his hinder parts. Uncle Rick was transformed into a flatfooted, overweight championship sprinter and was at least fifteen feet in front of us. We couldn't catch him. How was this possible? It was the adrenalin.

In times of crises, in the midnight hour the Holy Spirit raises up a standard by releasing large amounts of faith through the blood stream of Jesus. When we ought to die, we live. When we ought to quit, we go on. When the world thinks it's over, we walk on. Paul said in Galatians 2:20, "I am crucified with Christ: nevertheless I live; yet not I, but Christ liveth in me: and the life which I now live in the flesh I live by the faith of the Son of God, who loved me, and gave himself for me."

I've read the gripping, true stories of the early Church and how many Christians were martyred for the faith. Some were tortured and killed in the most horrible fashion. I have pondered in my heart how I would react if faced with execution at the chopping block, torture or imprisonment. My conclusion is that at that moment, God would release within my life what I would need to stand in that evil hour.

The great prophet Ezekiel was discouraged, down and depressed by the bondage of Israel in Babylon. What discouraged him the most was the apathy of his people. No one really cared. In the midnight hour of his lowest state a miracle took place. Ezekiel 2:2 states, "And the spirit entered into me when he spake unto me, and set me upon my feet . . ." When the enemy came in like a flood, the Spirit of the Lord raised up a standard! In times of danger, when things are against me, there is released in my spirit a faith to believe God for the impossible. What I cannot believe God for in ordinary times, I can believe Him for in times of crises. The three Hebrew boys, when faced with the fire and certain death, refused to bow to the golden idol. They stood there without a church and without a preacher. No angelic being came by to tell them, "If you don't bow God's going to keep you alive." No one wants to die. But God did release the faith they needed to stand in that desperate hour. There was faith to live or die. Their testimony was, "We don't know if we will be delivered, O king. We just know we're not going to bow!" When David faced Goliath his cry was, "Is there not a cause?" The Holy Spirit began to release into the little shepherd boy's spirit an influence called faith, and with a slingshot and rock he slaughtered the enemy.

We have all had to suffer the furnace of affliction and face the giant of intimidation, and no doubt will have to face and suffer them again. The midnight hour comes to all of us, and life gets turned upside down. But thanks be unto God for the faith of Jesus Christ. Where our faith is weak His faith is strong. His faith gives us buoyancy in the stormy waters of life. When you are a Christian, you're like a cat; you can be thrown upside-down, but you are always going to land on your feet. You're like a Timex watch; you can take a licking and keep on ticking. Jesus said in St. John, "In the world ye shall have tribulations, but be of good cheer I have overcome the world." You will have trouble as long as you are alive.

Remember you can't have a testimony without a test, nor can you have a crown without a cross. Don't let it get you down, but rather be of a joyful spirit because Jesus said, "I have overcome and, if I dwell in you, you will overcome too."

After almost eight years of pastoring my first church, I felt God was leading me in a new direction. My wife and I had been praying for a long time for the where and when. While I was away preaching a youth camp, my three most trusted leaders turned on me like Judas did on the Lord. When I returned, it hit me on the blind side. Instead of fighting with them I decided to resign and, like Abraham, I had no idea where I was going. Now the "when" was clear, but the "where" was foggy. I made a few phone calls to pastors I had promised to come and preach revivals for, so my calendar was filled for a few months. Surely within that time God would open a door for us to pastor again. I resigned on a Sunday and took a much-needed one-week vacation.

The following Saturday I broke my leg on a dirt bike trying to play Evel Knevel. My brothers, Tim and Todd loaded me up in the pickup and rushed me off to the hospital. We went by Tim's house on the way to tell my wife Keleta of the accident. As we pulled up in the driveway our wives were sitting in the garage, visiting. One of my brothers yelled out, "We are on our way to the hospital, Guy broke his leg." At first she didn't believe us. But when she got up and came to the window, looked in and saw me in pain beyond description, she believed. She broke down and started crying. This injury added to all we had just experienced was overwhelming. We were technically unemployed except for the revivals that I had scheduled. Now it would be impossibile for me to fulfill my commitments. I was facing surgery and months of therapy. The future never looked darker. She cried and asked me in a broken voice, "What are we going to do?" Before I had time to react the Spirit of the Lord rose up in me, and there was an extra amount of faith that was released. I looked deep into her eyes and with the confidence of God I told her, "The Lord has always been faithful, and I promise He will see us through." Understand this was not some flippant answer that just sounded good for the moment. This was an unshakable conviction that rose out of my soul that was born of the Holy Ghost. I knew everything was going to be all right. It was faith at the midnight hour. God is faithful. We never missed paying a bill on time!

In my life I have been lied about, slandered, betrayed, shot, stoned and left for dead in a spiritual sense. The devil said, "He'll never rise up again." That's when Christ's faith was released through me, and in my weakness I was made strong. By God's help I stood back up with my hands lifted high and I was able to sing, "It was grace that brought me safe thus far and grace will lead me home."

Church history tells the stirring story of the old preacher Polycarp, the bishop of Smyrna. He was tied to a stake with the threat of becoming a human torch if he did not recant his faith. His reply, "Eighty and six years have I served Him and He ain't never done me nothing but good!" To that they set him on fire and watched him burn. But the unthinkable happened—he wouldn't die. Like Paul and Silas, God gave Polycarp a song in the night, and he sang it out while the flesh melted from his bone. One of the soldiers couldn't take it any longer as conviction gripped his soul. He took a sword and thrust it through the old man of God and his blood put the fire out. The enemy came in like a flood, and the Spirit of the Lord raised up a standard.

Gideon and his three hundred mighty men had a possession that should stir your spirit, capture your imagination, and inspire your faith to the limits. The Bible says in Judges 8:4, "And Gideon came to Jordan, and passed over, he, and the three hundred men that were with him, faint, yet pursuing them." Those words, "faint, yet pursuing," have a wonderful message to every believer. They were tired and bone-weary, yet, something happened that was unexplainable—they never quit but rather keep pursuing the enemy. That is not natural; but, again, Christ's faith isn't natural—it's supernatural. Let the weak say, "I am strong." Let the poor say, "I am rich." Paul confessed his weakness as he wrestled with a thorn in the flesh, and asked the Lord three times to deliver him, yet, to his disappointment, all three times the answer was, "My grace is sufficient for thee: for my strength is made perfect in weakness." This set a resolve in Paul's heart that has forever been recorded in the Bible: "Most gladly therefore will I rather glory in my infirmities, that the power of Christ may rest upon me. Therefore I take pleasure in infirmities, in reproaches, in necessities, in persecutions, in distresses for Christ's sake: for when I am weak, then am I strong," (2 Corinthians 12:9-10). There have been times I felt I couldn't preach another sermon, pray another prayer, sing another song, or run another mile. I had fought my last battle, but I didn't give up, and somewhere out of nowhere came a second wind—the wind of God. And I keep pursuing. Christ's faith makes alive, it quickens, and breathes life back into dry bones. It revives zeal and causes mere mortals to talk and walk like God because God is not a quitter.

It is not what you do in times of great spiritual victory that will make you or break you; it is having the odds overwhelmingly against you that puts the proof in the pudding. The real man or woman doesn't stand up on the mountain when the victories are more than can be counted, and God's mighty presence is there to invigorate and empower you. It's not when you are winning a prodigious battle, but the real man stands up on his weakest day. The height of your heights will not determine your life, but rather, the height of your depths. How many lives have been wrecked and ruined in a time of weakness, all lost in one moment. Only the judgment will reveal how many lives could have risen like a mighty rocket soaring toward the heavens, but fell like a malfunction from Cape Canaveral all because of what they did in a time of weakness. There may have been hundreds of men just as powerful as D.L. Moody or John Wesley, who could have taken this world by storm but we will never hear from them because they gave up and lost it all in just five minutes. In their strength they could have matched any person on this earth; however, it wasn't what they could do on the mountaintop, it's what they did in their valleys, their depths, their weakness. What they did in the valley forfeited their right ever to ascend the peak of the mountain. What they did in the darkness forfeited their right to ever stand again in the bright lights of glory and victory. In those midnight hours when you are weak, for the sake of your soul, don't give up, but wait on the Lord and He will renew your strength, and like the Psalmist, "Weeping may endure for the night but joy cometh in the morning."

Before Christ's betrayal and crucifixion, He told Peter, "Satan hath desired to have you to sift you as wheat; but I have prayed for you that your faith will not fail." Jesus did not pray that Peter would not fall. In fact, He prophesied that he would when He told him, "The cock shall not crow this day until you have denied me three times." Jesus prayed that his faith would not fail. In Peter's falling late that night, in his sifting when fear has gripped his heart, when he's almost ready to give up, down deep inside faith like a generator starts going off that doesn't have anything to do with Peter. Suddenly he remembers the words of Jesus, "I have prayed for you that your faith will not fail."

Faith will not fail in the furnace. Faith will not fail in the flood. Faith will not fail in adversity when life is all mixed up. When you are falling and nobody's prayers seem to work, take on a new confidence, Jesus is praying for you that your faith will hold on through the midnight and make it to the morning. Now that's real faith!

Chapter
7

The Last Thread of Hope

*When she had heard of Jesus, came in the
press behind, and touched his garment.
For she said, if I may touch but his clothes,
I shall be whole.*

Mark 5:27-28

*J*esus said, "Who touched me?" That is a galvanizing
question when you realize who asked it and under what
conditions it was asked. You can't escape the rapture of it.
Excitement that grips you and holds you breathless when
you think of Christ, the Son of the living God stopping in
response to the touch of a destitute woman whose name we

are not told. "Who touched me?" Who, with an unshakable, unwavering, undisputed and unhindered faith touched me? Out of the thronging multitude Jesus recognized that one magnetic touch of faith. The touch of human faith—to stop, to halt, to make God aware of your problem, your pain, and your petition—has bold potential to arrest the Son of God. The heaviness of human suffering has always been a deep concern of the Almighty. For every adversity, He's got the answer and for every problem, He's got a promise. Yet, with every promise there is a condition. The multitude was pressing in on Him, and He was being touched from every side. But He only recognized one touch, the touch of real faith.

In this incredible but true story two faces emerge from the crowd, like watching an old black and white movie when to your amazement the two leading figures appear in real live Technicolor. They stand out and give the story the vivid detail of realism. There is the face of the Savior. It is His face that will draw and hold your gaze. One look on His face and your life will never be the same again. His is a face that will linger long in memory. It will refresh you long after the sun has gone down, and the black and cool night has stilled every noise in the metropolis, while only the celestial stars illuminate, like ten carat diamonds against black velvet. To see His face is not only to see the face of a man but to look on the face of God, the God of creation, compassion and everlasting love. To see the quality of His expression promises rest for the weary, sight for the blind, hope for the hurting, and triumph to those who have experienced the tragedies of life. Just one look offers healing for the spirit, soul, and body, forgiveness of sin and another chance. The penetration of His compassionate eyes seems to whisper a new beginning, a fresh and new tomorrow in which there will be no more suffering, pain, disease, neglect, hunger, broken dreams, nor death.

Then, there is the face of the woman: It is a face that portrays great depth of human emotion and agony, a face that was once beautiful and imaged the look of innocence. With cheeks of red and starlit eyes her countenance was as fresh as the morning. When she walked into the room, the beauty of her face demanded attention, for her look was stunning. But, that was before her blood was an issue. Now her face reflected the agony of the pain of twelve long years of acute suffering. From out of nowhere came the malady of cancer of the blood. Her natural beauty was marred by the torment of perpetual misery. The hemorrhage would not go away. She went to physician after physician and found no cure, but, rather, grew worse. She disbursed her life's savings. Every day was another hopeless sunrise. The words "incurable" and "terminal" seem to be in every conversation as a constant reminder there may never be a tomorrow.

She is a nameless woman with a lethal blood disease. Why doesn't the Bible tell us her name? It is simple because she embodies the incalculable cases of endless pain and human hopelessness. The world couldn't help her nor bring any kind of healing. She was running out of time, for every stroke of the clock brought her closer to that dreaded hour of demise. She had spent sleepless days and sleepless nights. The last ray of hope had already gone down behind the hill of despair. She was down to her last thread. There was one plan left, "If I may touch but His clothes, I shall be whole."

As that revelation burned in her heart, it suspended the machinery of her mind. The pageantry of that conviction transcended every other thought. Her faith was dramatically stirred. So, she came in the press, and, when she got close enough, she reached through, with a trembling finger and touched but the threads of his clothes. That's all it took! With the impact of divine vitality there surged life back into her infected veins, and the origin of her bloody contamination was dried up. The threatening terminal disease was crushed in one deadening blow. Once again, the Great Physician resurrected life and gave hope in what the world called an irreversible situation. Faith was the last thread of hope, and it held.

Faith in God has not changed because God has not changed. Isn't it good to know that in a world of cataclysmic and constant change, God remains the same? He won't be Deliverer one day and Denier the next. He won't pull you up one day and then push you down the next. He won't gather you in one day then cast you out the next. Jesus Christ is the same from everlasting to everlasting. The Apostle Paul picked up on this when he wrote, "Jesus Christ the same yesterday, and today, and for ever." This is one anchor you can hold on to in the midst of the quicksand of your circumstance. You may be up today and down tomorrow. You may be feasting today and fasting tomorrow. Friends come in your life and out of your life. In one day you can go from the palace to the pit, have it all but in one fleeting moment have nothing. When all hope dissipates like dew off the rose bud, you can count on and take to the bank the consistency of God. God will not change! The threads of faith are as solid as the Rock of Ages.

The Four Threads of Faith

1. She Heard

Paul tells us in Romans 10:17, "So then faith cometh by hearing, and hearing by the Word of God." This woman with the issue of blood heard the lepers tell of their miraculous cure. She heard one man tell that from birth he had lived in total eclipse without any hope of day. But, one afternoon Jesus of Nazareth passed by and called his name. In an instant grace shattered the pessimism of thirty-eight years of total blindness. Jesus cast the door open, and the man stepped into the light. That was the day he threw down his cup and his cane. He was a new man all because of the one they call Jesus; that's what she heard. She listened to the deaf recite in detail the wonders of hearing the songbird sing in the misty morning for the first time. People with crooked limbs and withered hands testified of the miraculous. Their eyes flashed and filled with tears as they told their almost unbelievable but true stories. She heard what He had done for others. Surely if He did that for them, He would do it for her. Surely He had the power to raise from the dregs of disease the flowers whose petals had been crushed, whose stems had been broken, and whose hopes had been withered in the furnace of affliction.

Do you want to hear something that will build your faith with a life-changing dimension? Isaiah, the Old Testament prophet, said in chapter 53, verse 4, "Surely he hath borne our griefs, and carried our sorrows." He said SURELY! Just as sure as the sun will come up in the morning and just as sure as the ocean will not evaporate, the death, burial and resurrection of Jesus Christ are a fact and not fantasy. "He was wounded for our transgressions; he was bruised for our iniquities: the chastisement of our peace was upon him; and with his stripes we are healed."

2. She Came

Why is it that at the first sign of trouble we have a human weakness to run? I have had people tell me, "Things are so bad in my life I believe I'll just backslide." God expects us to use our head for something more than to separate our ears. That would be like a soldier saying, "I am sick of war, so I believe I will just quit and turn myself over to the enemy." If you like hanging out in concentration camps and having bamboo shoved up your fingernails, go ahead and throw down your gun. However, I have a strong suggestion for you: Don't throw down your weapon. Don't discard the cross and cast your commitment aside like a dirty garment. Pick up that cross and come running to Jesus. When you've tried everything else and can't get any relief, read all the books and still don't have the answer, gone to all the seminars, talked to all the counselors, and spent all your money, and you are still not any better, do what this little lady did and come to Jesus. He's still the Answer. She came and found the answer! The answer to man's most perplexing problems is not found in a pill or liquor bottle. Being drugged or drunk is not the answer. Backsliding, suicide or sex is not the answer. Jesus Christ the Son of the living God is still the answer even after the changing of two millenniums. Come to Him!

3. She Said

Literally this woman "said" within her self; in other words, she had a habit of talking to herself. Do you ever talk to yourself? Sure you do and every day. You either talk to yourself in a negative way, or you speak to yourself in the positive mode. Some people say, "I knew it wouldn't work out; everything I touch falls apart." That's not faith. She said to herself, "I know, if I can but touch His clothes, I can be made whole." She didn't take a poll or wait on a vote. She didn't call old granny grunt and ask her what she thought about it. No one was going to stand in her way, and no one was going to talk her out of it. You can't talk to God until you first talk to yourself. You have got to be like the prodigal son and say, "Self, what are you doing in this hog pen?" Luke 15:17 records, "And when he came to himself, **he said**, 'How many hired servants of my father's have bread enough and to spare, and I perish with hunger! I will arise and go to my father, and will say unto him, Father; I have sinned against heaven, and before thee.'" Say to yourself, "Self, what are you doing here about to have a nervous breakdown?" "What am I doing here with these divorce papers in my hand?" "Why are my children lost?" "Self, why do you allow these thoughts of suicide run through your head? I shall be whole!"

4. She Touched

In 1987 I attended a large preacher's conference in Oklahoma City. There were over fifteen thousand people in attendance. I was a twenty-four year old full-time evangelist.

As I sat there in my seat, I casually turned and looked behind me before the service started. To my shock, sitting behind me within twenty feet was the biggest television preacher (at that time) in the world. His was a household name. From the first time I heard him on television I was driven with a secret desire to preach and be just like him. He was my hero and role model in life. I couldn't believe that by chance I had sat so close to him. To me he was bigger than life. Just to think there was a great possibility I was even going to have the good fortune to meet him, or at least shake his hand. As the service progressed I formulated my plan, which was quite simple: He had to walk by me so there was no way he could escape. At the end of service, a service from which I received nothing because I was so caught up with meeting this great preacher, we all stood to be dismissed. I never took my eyes off him. He came down the stairs, mobbed by those around him. He was shaking hands like a celebrity from Hollywood. He was two steps up and two feet away while my heart was beating with anticipation. He shook another hand then turned to walk on down the steps. He was directly in front of me now. I reached my hand out to shake his, but he never looked at me; he kept walking. My mind was racing with the thought, "I will never be any closer. It looks as though he will disappear into the crowd, and I will never get another chance." So at that point, without thinking, I reached out and grabbed him by the arm. He never turned to look at me and never broke stride. He just brushed my hand free, and in seconds he was gone. Needless to say, my feelings were devastated. In my mind the great evangelist rejected me.

Not long after, while I was in prayer, the Lord replayed

that scene and gave me a spiritual application. I touched a man and nothing happened. He never even took the time to look at me. Though great in my eyes, he was still just a man. But the Lord is not just a man. He is God and He loves me. If I will touch Him, He will stand still and take time for me.

This little lady had to push her way through the mob-like crowd, growing ever closer to Jesus. She was down to her last thread and it was getting more ragged by the moment. It seemed that every obstacle and hindrance were present, to discourage and stop her. She must touch Him. She struggled through the compacted crowd like a salmon swimming upstream against all odds. She was pushed down, pushed away, and pushed aside, but she would not give up. Finally, the poor woman drew near enough that she reached through and with a quivering finger she touched just the threads of His robe, and like turning on the light in a dark room, the healing came and dispelled every trace of the darkness of her dreaded disease. She was healed, and her issue of blood was not an issue any more.

Chapter
8

Losing Faith with the Taste of Fish Still in Your Mouth

For they considered not the miracle of the loaves: for their heart was hardened.

Mark 6:52

*L*ife has its storms. The fact is you are either in a storm, coming out of a storm, or you are on the glassy perimeter of your next storm. And, life goes from calm to chaos in just a matter of minutes. Then here comes the big question: "Where on earth is the Lord when I am in the storm?" "Where is God when I'm lonely?" "Where is He when I'm discouraged and down and out?" "Where in the world is my personal Savior when my lifeboat springs a leak? When my parachute won't open? When my brakes go out on the avenue of life? When the last dollar is gone before the last bill is paid and the last hope leaves on the last train, where is God?" But, the answer to this question is really quite simple. It can be answered with a question, "Where is God not?" An atheist once asked a little boy who had just come from Sunday school where God was. He told the boy, if he could answer the question correctly, he would give him a brand new, shiny dime. Quick as a flash his answer came and his voice was not faint, "I'll give you a dollar, mister, if you will tell me where God ain't."

"And he saw them toiling in rowing; for the wind was contrary unto them," (Mark 6:48). You are in the eye of the storm. God is omnipresent. To a student of theology that means He is everywhere at all times. But to the Christian who has experienced the storms of life, it takes on a much more personal meaning. If I go through the valley of the shadow of death, "Thou art with me." When I walk down the avenue of adversity, He is there. When I sail into the sea of sorrow, He is there. When I get swept down a river of ridicule or caught up in a hurricane from hell, He is always present with me. He has made us this promise, "Lo, I am with you always, even unto the end of the world. Amen," (Matthew 28:20).

Did you ever notice before the storm of God's judgment struck this world in the form of a flood, what the Lord told Noah? He simply said, "Noah, you and your family come into the ark." On the surface there is nothing there but with a closer examination the truth emerges. God did not say, "Noah, get into the ark," but "Come into the ark." God was in the ark! Christ is in your storm! He not only sees what you feel but He feels what you feel because He is with you.

A little boy was eagerly looking forward to the birthday party of a friend who lived only a few blocks away. When the day arrived, a blizzard made the sidewalks and roads nearly impassible. The lad's father, sensing the danger, hesitated to let his son go. The youngster reacted tearfully. "But Dad," he pleaded, "all the other kids will be there. Their parents are letting them go." The father thought for a minute, then replied softly, "All right, you may go." Surprised but overjoyed, the boy bundled up and plunged into the raging storm. The driving snow made visibility almost impossible, and it took him more than half an hour to trudge the short distance to the party. As he rang the doorbell, he turned briefly to look out into the storm. His eye caught the shadow of a retreating figure. It was his father. He had followed his son's every step to make sure he arrived safely.

By the age of 11, my daughter Shanta had developed a non-life-threatening tumor which had to be removed from the bone in her knee. The day had come, and we found ourselves walking beside her rolling bed on the way to the surgery room. We walked as far as they would allow, and we were stopped by a door. Keleta and I kissed our little angel and told her we would be in the waiting room. Through the door she went and down the hall. We watched through the door window until she turned the corner out of our sight and into the hands of the caring surgeon. Our hearts sank and a river of emotions flooded our eyes. We felt so helpless. We had to stop at the door. But I can tell you Christ did not stop at the door! He is the Door and He walks through doors. Doors, devils, and demons can't stop Him. Atheists, agnostics, and attitudes can't stop Him. Sin and storms can't stop the Son of God, for He walks on storms and whispers, "Peace, be still," and they must obey Him. You can only go so far; He can go farther. You can pray only so hard; He can pray harder. You can only say so much; He can say more. You are limited, but He is unlimited. You are hindered by time, space and strength, but He is all-knowing, all-powerful, all-sufficient and all-present. Jesus is all-God!

One dark night after everyone in the house was asleep, a storm rolled in with a threatening howl. The lightning was flashing giving a lighted aerial display to the point of causing the neighborhood security lights to retire for the night in their vigil watch. The thunder was crashing like the German blitz over London, England, rattling every window with its constant boom. Suddenly my youngest son Simeon came bolting into my room, jumped up in my bed, threw his little arms around my neck, and with a trace of terror in his voice said, "Daddy, would you pray, now?" I started praying, and, when I was through with my prayer, the little Guy (the pun was intended) was sound asleep. If in the storm you feel the least bit threatened, I suggest you run to the Lord for He is praying for you, and He is with you while He prays.

The story of the disciples in the storm both amazes and amuses me. It is the mirror of life. Just a few hours before the storm, the twelve had witnessed the awesome display of God's creative power. Jesus with two fish and five loaves had fed five thousand plus people. Let's be real. This was no ordinary run-of-the-mill type of deal. Those kinds of things don't happen just every Monday. Not only did these men witness the miracle, but they also took part and participated in it. Now, as they are in the storm, their minds have a senior moment, and they get a bad case of amnesia. The miracle of the feeding of the five thousand is quickly forgotten as the gale force winds blow violently against the ship. With the taste of fish still in their mouths, they lost their faith.

When you lose your faith, you get desperately overwhelmed with the circumstance. Life becomes as complicated as an airplane cockpit. You don't know what button to push or lever to flip. Bailing out seems to be the best option. But, abandoning the ship is not God's plan for your life. He wants you to stay in the boat and stay steady and balanced. His purpose is for your faith to grow. When we are in the storm our natural reaction is, "This is of the devil." But, let us not forget it was God's will those disciples were on the boat in the storm. "And straightway he constrained his disciples to get into the ship, and to go to the other side," (Mark 6:45). That was His will; so, there is no way we can go under for going over! How many times has God worked a miracle in our life, and with the taste of fish still fresh in our mouth, bread still in our teeth and the memory of the miracle still crisp on our mind, we lose our faith? We get caught up in the storm and forget everything we have ever sung or testified about. We forget every promise in the Bible and vacillate between fear and faith until we totally lose every ounce of faith we possess and feel as though Christ has left us alone.

Once there was a little feisty dog about the size of a number eleven shoe who set his throne up on the porch of his master's home. A chain link fence dictated his domain. He kept a constant patrol of his kingdom walking with the confidence of an attack dog along the inside perimeter of the fence. When an intruder walked along the outside of the fence, man or beast, he, with his extroverted personality, let them know with what he considered a ferocious bark that they were walking on dangerous ground. And he would not let up until they were out of view. One day two Doberman Pinschers at least five times his size came along the fence. He came running off the porch in a command performance, hit the gate, and yelped until they passed. They paid no attention to the pint size want-to-be Rin Tin Tin. This scene became a daily ritual for at the same time every day the two Dobermans came cruising. The little dog was only a small announce to the much bigger dogs until one day he came charging off the porch. When he hit the gate, it opened and he went tumbling out of the fence to find himself lodged under the biggest dog. Those two dogs turned him every which way but loose until finally he got free. He ran back through the gate, hit the porch, slid into his dog house and turned to see his victorious enemy glide proudly out of sight, then with a loud voice of disgust asked, "Who's the fool that left the gate open?" He was a legend in his own mind behind the safety of the fence. He had courage and faith as long as he was behind the gate. However, when he got into the real arena of battle he lost it all.

A lot of people can talk a big faith inside the fence with the gate locked. They feel secure within the hedge. But what happens when the hedge is let down, and, like Job, they don't have the security of the fence any longer? I know what some do. They run like a scared Chihuahua back to the porch yelling, "Oh, God, oh, God, oh, God!" If you can't run with the big dogs, you'd better stay on the porch! If you can't handle the storm, you'd better not get in the boat. But if you don't get in the boat, don't ever expect to get to the other side. God wants you on the other side. There are three primary reasons why we lose our faith:

1. We Fail to Educate Our Faith

To fail in the education of your mind is a human tragedy. You limit so many wonderful possibilities in life. If you never learn the basic principles of reading, writing, and arithmetic, you are faced with a major handicap. Education is imperative in order to be a functioning citizen of society. Otherwise, you are destined to live on a lower plane. We by the grace of God have educated ourselves out of polio, smallpox, and other diseases that threatened our mortality. Yet there is one disease that x-rays and neurosurgeons can't detect. It doesn't show up in human DNA. The disease of unbelief is implicitly lethal to the immortal soul. Unless you educate your faith and stay in a perpetual learning mode you will spiritually die.

Because of unbelief, Demas forsook the Apostle Paul, even after being involved with his powerful and miraculous ministry. Judas walked away from his faith after witnessing every miracle that the Lord performed from the turning of the water into wine to raising a four-day-dead Lazarus from the grave. In the Old Testament it is recorded that a whole generation of Israelites died in the wilderness after seeing and authenticating every kind of miracle imaginable. Paul told Timothy, "Study to show thyself approved unto God, a workman that needeth not to be ashamed, rightly dividing the word of truth," (2 Timothy 2:15).

2. We Fail to Exercise Our Faith

What happens when we don't exercise our bodies? We get weak, frail and sickly. Medical science tells us, if the heart muscle doesn't receive the proper workout, with time it can develop a multiplicity of problems. Hardening of the arteries is one of the more common. "For they considered not the miracle of the loaves: for their heart was hardened," (Mark 6:52).

The long feared drought had finally come to Delta County. On Sunday morning the preacher petitioned his parishioners to pray and have faith in God to break the drought. He explained in his usual prophetic tone that God still worked miracles and faith still moved mountains. Then he called the congregation to the altar for a time of corporate prayer. Later that same day, as the members were gathering for the evening service, one dear saint was seen coming inside the church carrying an umbrella. Since there wasn't a cloud in the sky, and they were in the middle of a drought, this seemed rather humorous to the people and especially to the pastor. So the pastor asked the lady why she brought her umbrella to church. To the question she answered, "Well, I thought we were praying for rain!"

To build and maintain a healthy faith you have got to

exercise it. "But ye, beloved, building up yourselves on your most holy faith, praying in the Holy Ghost," (Jude 1:20). You have to pray and stretch your faith even when you don't feel like it. Give to God when you can't afford it. No pain no gain.

3. We Fail to Enjoy Our Faith

The disciples lost their joy in faith for Mark 6:48 says, "Jesus saw them toiling in rowing." Their rowing became toil. In other words, their rowing was reduced to work and labor; the fun was gone. As they started out across that placid lake, their faith was ecstatic with thrill. To be an eye-witness would have been enough, but to actually be a part of the most phenomenal working of the supernatural ever manifested was beyond description. No doubt, this man Jesus was the Son of God, and if He could feed over five thousand people with a little lad's lunch, He could do anything. Their faith was at peak as joy overflowed from the cup of human experience. But, in a matter of minutes the sky grew dark, and the waves started slapping the side of the boat with a thunderous crash. Their faith was replaced by fear as they lost all their expectation. Now, on the ragged edge of life faith seemed a forgotten fantasy. The storm took the shining luster out of their miraculous experience.

If you are not careful, the storms that blow against your life will wipe your memory bank clean and cause your spiritual hard drive to crash, leaving you without faith, joy and hope. Storms have a way of taking the joy out of faith, of taking the clap out of your hands, and of taking the dance out of your feet and the praise out of your mouth. Storms will either push you away from God or draw you near to Him. The old adage, "The same sun that melts wax hardens clay," is true to life. When the gale force winds explode with a vengeance, your spiritual life will either deepen with experience, or it will be uprooted with the encounter. Tribulation adds a greater depth of dimension to our lives. An old Arabian proverb says simply, "All sunshine makes a desert." They ought to know. When life is easy, it is possible to live on the surface, but, when trial and sorrow comes, it drives us to deeper things. God's rainbow is in the storm!

Where did John receive the Revelation of Jesus Christ? It wasn't on the golf course, nor was it while he was on a two week vacation to Tahiti. He was on the isle of Patmos, which wasn't a tropical paradise but an island so forsaken and desolate that only the most hardened criminals were placed there. God can grow a mushroom overnight, but it takes many years and many storms to grow a mighty oak. Life's greatest revelations come through tribulations. Growing above the timberline are the trees that produce the most exquisite grain and resonant wood. Their secret is deeper roots to endure the stress of high winds and storms. God so meticulously provided for the strain. An extra flow of resin is produced that gives them the elegant grain from which the finest musical instruments in the world are made, instruments that in turn have blessed thousands of lives and calmed many a troubled heart and stressed mind. God's choicest saints, those who have the greatest texture and who give the world its most inspiring songs, are the same ones who have endured some of the greatest strains and winds of adversity. Fanny Crosby was sentenced to live almost a lifetime of blindness, yet God gave her an enduring song that has blessed multitudes.

Take away the pain and isolation, and you will take away the Bedford dungeon from John Bunyan, but in the process you will also take away the classic, *Pilgrims Progress* out of every library in the world. Take away the cross from Jesus, and you will have sealed the destiny of every human being that has ever had hope beyond the grave. It takes strength formed in the furnace of agony. "Without shedding of blood is no remission of sin," (Hebrews 9:22). There is no salvation without the cross, and there is no strength without the storm. One explorer in the year 1520 wrote in his memoirs, "The Sea is dangerous and its storms terrible, but these obstacles have never been sufficient reason to stay ashore." Jesus told His disciples to get in the boat and cross to the other side and, in essence, this is His command to us. Don't forget all the miracles God has done in your life the next time you are faced with the stress of the storm. Hold on to your faith, and it will see you through safely. And remember, you can't go under for going over!

Chapter
9

In the Presence of the Enemy

*Thou preparest a table before me
in the presence of mine enemies:*

Psalms 23:5

No one likes an enemy, but, unfortunately, somewhere along the long and winding road of human experience we all have gained one or two. You said or did something that rubbed someone else the wrong way. No doubt, even after all these years you are still on someone's hit list. I once knew a man that had so much dislike for another fellow that he literally cut his picture out of his own high school yearbook. But life took a twist of irony, for in later years the enemy that had been surgically removed from the book became this man's pastor. Hate dissolved into love and the enemy became a friend and faithful shepherd. A little girl was disciplined by her parents, and for her actions she was made to sit at a small card table for supper all by herself. To add to her punishment she was called on to pray and ask the grace over the meal. She bowed her head and prayed, "Thank you, Lord, for you are so kind that thou preparest a table before me in the presence of my enemies, amen!"

Every Christian has a common enemy. Guess who it is? Not one another. It is not a political party nor is it another race of people; it is the devil. Satan is your enemy. One of the greatest secrets to living a victorious and overcoming Christian life is to realize there is an enemy that will throw us into spiritual conflict. It is a combat that is more hostile and dangerous than Vietnam. What is at stake is not lands, kingdoms, or treasures, but the human soul of mankind. Your eternal soul is at risk.

The enemy usually approaches at your weakest moment. During times of weakness and crisis, the enemy moves in with unsportsmanlike conduct. He seeks a crack in the wall to set up a stronghold. The atmosphere is infested with lying, deceitful spirits that are bent on one objective, our destruction. Why do you think it's so hard to pray? Why do you think, when you start a fast, someone inevitably will call or drop by and offer to take you out to eat? Why is Sunday the hardest day of the week to get up on? Have you ever noticed that on Saturday night it seems that every dog in the neighborhood goes into a barking fit? You usually get more wrong number phone calls after 12:00 midnight; the faucet drips; the commode seeps, and the walls creak on Saturday night. Why? Because it is just another ploy of the enemy to keep you up so that come Sunday morning, you are drained and so tired you can't even stay awake (if you even go to church) during the pastor's message. The devil doesn't want you to hear the Word because "faith cometh by hearing, and hearing by the Word of God." That Word will set you free and lay out a table for you right in full view of the enemy!

In St. Luke, Chapter 11, Jesus cast the devil out of a dumb man, and, when he spoke, the people were in wonder. But, some of them said, "He casteth out devils through Beelzebub, the chief of the devils." Jesus then discoursed on the disruptive manner of Satan, his kingdom, and the devastating effect of division. Then he added this telling statement: "But if I with the finger of God cast out devils, no doubt the kingdom of God is come upon you." In the Word of God there is the arm of God, the hand of God, and the finger of God. Jesus says that all He has to use is the finger of God to cast the enemy out.

You, as a believer, have all authority that Christ has given. It doesn't require the arm of God or the hand of God just the finger of God functioning in your life for you to live a victorious Christian life. Most people have had a fight at some time in their lives—not just an argument but a real rough and tumble fist fight. While time seemed to stop and the environment had ground down to slow motion, your adrenalin was in high gear, and the person you were fighting became the enemy. With tunnel vision you clenched your fist tight, and with your hands and your arms you stepped into battle. I never witnessed a fight where the two opponents fought while one only used just a single finger.

A man died and was ushered to the pearly gates of heaven. St. Peter asked but one question to the man: "Did you ever do anything good in your entire life?" The man replied, "As a matter of fact, I did. Once there was a motor-cycle gang harassing a very elderly woman and I walked into the middle of them and punched the ruthless, low-down leader right square in the nose." St. Peter, looking very puzzled, asked, "When did this take place?" The man replied, "Five minutes ago!" If you jump in to fight with just one finger, you will probably be looking at the pearly gates in five minutes too. That's your finger, but with the finger of God you can get the supernatural enemy under control.

The New Testament book of Colossians, Chapter 2:15 states: "And having spoiled principalities and powers, he made a show of them openly, triumphing over them in it." Study these four key words: 1) **Spoiled**: To take or strip from the enemy all authority, power, wealth and goods. 2) **Show**: To put on display; to display as in a window. 3) **Openly**: In full view of everyone. 4) **Triumphing**: To cele-brate a triumph in the presence of the enemy.

After a Roman conquest, the victorious general would lead a triumphal procession through the streets of Rome leading his vanquished enemy and all his spoil. Tens of thousands of Roman citizens, in celebration along the streets, cheered, threw confetti, and waved banners in trib-ute of the great general and his winning army. It was the father of the ticker tape parade given in honor of a hero in New York City. After the march the general and all of his officers were lionized with a colossal feast given by the Emperor himself. To enhance the victory the leading captives such as the king, the generals, and any dignitaries were brought into the banquet hall and chained to the pillars. There the conquerors would drink and feast in celebration while the enemy gnashed their teeth in helpless rage and tugged at the chains that held them captive. What a poignant picture!

"Thou preparest a table before me in the presence of mine enemies!" Look at them now and see the antagonistic glare in their hateful eyes. Fear, temptation, sin, and even the devil himself have been chained to the pillars of truth. They wrench and hiss, "Just wait. We will have you eventually." But don't be afraid. Relax and enjoy the celebration. Find added passion, spice, and relish in the cup of salvation. Discover additional enhancement in the bread of life. Sit up closer to God's divine table. Get snug as a bug in a rug to Christ the Mighty Conqueror. No weapon formed against you shall prosper. Not one hair on your head shall perish. Right in the presence of the enemy we share in the greatest victory of the universe. We are made more than conquerors through Jesus Christ our Lord!

The faith of one, certain disabled woman was so strong she believed that if God fed the prophet Elijah by ravens from Ahab's table, He was certainly capable in doing it again. Many times she prayed her next meal in. She awoke one morning to discover she was out of food, so without hesitation she got down on her arthritic knees and petitioned the

Lord for help. She lived in a duplex apartment and on the other side of the wall lived an atheist. Every morning and every night he was in deep annoyance of this praying woman's prayers. This particular morning he heard her praying for groceries. So he schemed what he thought was a great plan to show this woman how ridiculous faith was in a God you could not see. He hurriedly raced to the local grocery store and bought a big bill of groceries. Once he was home he sneaked over and placed the many sacks at her doorstep, rang her doorbell, then hid in the shrubs to see her reaction. When this godly woman opened the door and saw the abundant supply of food, she threw her hands up in the air and cried, "Praise God, praise God. Lord, you done went and done it again. Praise God!" This really disturbed the atheist because he was the one who bought the groceries, and yet God was getting the credit. He bolted out of the shrubs and declared to the woman in no uncertain terms that God had nothing to do with this. It wasn't a miracle after all because he went in his car, spent his money, put the bags on her front porch, and rang the doorbell himself; thus, God was not to get the tribute. She threw her hands up again and with even more excitement professed her faith in Christ by crying, "Praise God, praise God. Lord, you done went and done it again. Yes, Lord, you done it again, and this time you made the devil pay for it!"

No matter what the circumstances, if God wants to, He can even use the devil to pay for it. How many churches have been built by unbelievers? How many ministries have been funded by men who never darken the door of a church? When Moses and the Israelites left out of Egypt, they took with them the best sheep, cattle, and all sorts of livestock. They took with them stockpiles of gold, silver, and precious gems. Pharaoh didn't want to let them go, but, God squeezed the Imperial Potentate's heart, and, when God got through with him, he not only let them go but also sponsored the trip!

In the mid 1990's, while pastoring my first church, we had a split. I watched half of our church's income get up and walk out one Sunday night. The future looked very uncertain and from the human perspective the word "hopeless" was inscribed over the door. But, God came to remind us He was still in control, and it was His Church and the gates of hell could not prevail. He took His divine inscriber and erased the "less" we had lost and left us with "hope." One day shortly after the sudden reduction in size and finance we received a very healthy check in the mail from a man who didn't even go to church. I visited him to thank him and to make sure it wasn't a mistake. Did I mention I was God's man of faith and power in those days? This man didn't make a mistake, and he knew nothing about the church split. One day God impressed him that he needed to honor God with his tithes even though he was not a Christian. From that day until the church got on its feet he sent his tithes like clockwork. More money came from here and there, and we never went in the red. The first year after the pruning we were in the black one hundred dollars! God was faithful!

The same God who gave the invocation at the dawn of creation is the same God who will give the benediction at the twilight of history! How many times has God blessed His people in the presence of the enemy? He blessed Moses in the presence of Pharaoh.

He blessed Samson in the presence of the Philistines.

He blessed Gideon in the presence of the Midianites.

He blessed David in the presence of Goliath.

He blessed Elijah in the presence of all the
prophets of Baal.

He blessed Daniel in the presence of his
lying adversaries.

God blessed the early church in spite of the coliseums, the lions, and gladiators, the fires of Nero and all the imperial powers of Rome. All the fury and ferocity of hell came against God's people. The Church stood like a branch against the mighty Niagara. But, when the dust had settled and the smoke had cleared, the Church was still standing, and all her enemies were on their knees.

Need I remind you that you, my friend, are the apple of God's eye? That is the most sensitive part of your body. You may let someone touch your forehead, punch you in the arm, hit you in the chest, step on your foot, pull your nose, or thump you on the ear. But, it will be a cold day in July before you let someone touch your eye. You will guard it, protect it, and even, subconsciously, keep a restrictive watch over it. You are the most sensitive part of God's creation. The enemy can destroy the trees, the fish, the fowl, and even burn a hole in the ozone, but the devil can not destroy you. God told Satan, when speaking of Job, "Behold, all that he hath is in thy power; only upon himself put not forth thine hand," (Job 1:12). If you have been blood bought, you belong to God; you are not your own anymore. The enemy may try everything to destroy your life. You may be in the middle of an onslaught of fiery darts, but, when it's all over and the victory has been won, God is going to throw the golden cloth over heaven's table, and He is going to pour you out a blessing right in the presence of your enemies. "So the Lord blessed the latter end of Job more than his beginning," (Job 42:12). God did it again.

Chapter
10

Born for Battle

Hast thou given the horse strength?
Hast thou clothed his neck with thunder?
Canst thou make him afraid as a grasshopper?
The glory of his nostrils is terrible.
He paweth in the valley, and rejoiceth in his strength:
he goeth on to meet the armed men.
He mocketh at fear, and is not affrighted;
neither turneth he back from the sword.
The quiver rattleth against him,
the glittering spear and the shield.
He swalloweth the ground with fierceness and rage:
neither believeth he that it is the sound of the trumpet.
He saith among the trumpets, Ha, ha;

and he smelleth the battle afar off,
the thunder of the captains, and the shouting.

Job 39:19-25

*W*ouldn't it be nice if every day you awoke from the peace of tranquility, that your sleeping chamber was illuminated with the vibrant iridescent colors of the rainbow? The smell of frankincense and cinnamon could be smelled in every fiber in the room. A celestial symphony played a gentle anthem of enchantment while a soft, cool breeze from paradise blew through your window ever so gently. A quartet of angels unfurled their wings and stepped to the side of your bed with the solemn promise, "Whatever you need today, we are here." You could arise and brush back the silk curtain, look into heaven, and see Jesus standing at the right hand of the Father giving you the personal thumbs-up sign. Then you could read His lips "Don't worry my child. I am with you, and you are going to make it today." What a way to start your day! I don't know about you, but my usual day or even my unusual day has never started with such exhilarating confidence. There have been those times when I awoke with only one question, "How in the world did that 18-wheeler drive over the top of me, and it didn't wake me up?" I felt as though I had been hit by a Mac truck. Most of my days start and finish in a foxhole. Life is a battle!

Job writes of the war horse and his battles and; it is evident he was born for battle, and so were you. Sam Jones, a great preacher from another century, knew this, and it is reflected in his prayer:

*"Lord, put plenty of knowledge in the gable of my
soul. Give me a back-bone like a saw log and a
rhinoceros hide for skin. Lord, put iron in my shoes
and give me a pair of galvanized britches. Help
me to sign a contract to fight the devil with my fist,
bite him till I ain't got no teeth and then gum him
till I die!"*

The apostle Paul wrote young Timothy and encouraged
him to,

*"Endure hardness, as a good soldier of Jesus
Christ," (2 Timothy 2:3). "This charge I commit
unto thee, son Timothy, according to the prophe-
cies which went before on thee, that thou by them
mightest war a good warfare," (1 Timothy 1:18).
"Fight the good fight of faith, lay hold on eternal
life, whereunto thou art also called, and hast professed a good profession before many witnesses,"
(1 Timothy 6:12)*

The moment you were saved and received eternal salvation you were thrown into the battle. You may have hoped
for a more positive outlook on life, but the Bible bears it out,
you were born for battle.

God took our physical body and designed it to withstand
the onslaught of a fallen world to give us a spiritual lesson
in survival. Almost every vital organ of the human anatomy
is protected by a shield of bone. We have present within our
body a standing army of white corpuscles. When we cut

ourselves, they march out to the sound of the ram's horn just as Israel did many millennia ago. They march out to fight and do warfare with the invading lethal bacteria. If those platelets of divine intervention had been left out in the creation, we all would have died a long time ago with gangrene. God placed within the human spirit the determining factor that is commonly called "self preservation," the drive to go on in spite of almost insurmountable circumstance. How many stories have we read that testify to the resiliency of the human spirit, stories of individuals who braved the blitz of earth's elements and lived to tell the story.

On April 10, 1942, General Douglas Macarthur had to evacuate the Philippine Islands, leaving his tired army there to face the swelling tide of the enemy. In a matter of weeks it was all over. The Japanese took the Islands, and the American soldiers who were left became prisoners of war. My step-grandfather, Clint Brewer, was one of the many thousands in the infamous "Bataan death march." A sixty-five mile, grueling march under the most agonizing heat fabricated by the Filipino sun. Humidity was so thick you could have cut it with a knife. Men fell like flies as the intensity of the sun grew hotter. They were denied food and water. Their personal possessions and equipment were stripped from them. They were hungry, thirsty, and bone weary, driven like cattle to the slaughter. Along the way they were beaten, clubbed, and bayoneted. If a soldier fell and couldn't get back up before the guard reached him, he was either shot or thrust through with a Japanese bayonet and left to die. It was like a horrible nightmare from which there was no waking. The record stands for the whole world to see: Seventy-eight thousand started the march, fifty-four thousand made it to the prison camps. For the next three years many more died at the hands of the Japanese. Medical care was non-existent. There were no toilet facilities, and, because of dysentery, the camps were soon covered with excrement. Starvation, malnutrition, dysentery, and malaria took their deadly toll. When the war started my grandfather weighed around two hundred pounds, but after he and the others were rescued, he weighed eighty pounds. I sat with him for two hours one blistering, hot July day and listened to his terrifying true story of survival. I hung on his every word, gripped in the tragedy of human suffering. The lesson I learned that not so distant summer day was clear, "It's not how big the boy is in the fight, but it's how big the fight is in the boy."

God made us to win and overcome the bitterness of spiritual warfare. Job dips the brush of his verbal artistry and paints us a picture of life in vivid detail in that of the warhorse. He describes this horse until you can almost hear the grinding of the bit, and the clatter of his hoofs among the fallen shields. Job said, "He paweth in the valley." The horse paws for one reason; the adrenaline flows to his feet, and he is ready to go to battle. As the warriors clad in battle armor mount their gallant steeds, a sense of arrogance radiates from these powerful animals. The long flowing mane is an icon of pride. You can't make him afraid like a grasshopper. His majestic snorting strikes terror in the enemy. He smells the blood and sweat of the battle from afar. The captains shout out their orders while the trumpeters blow their trumpets. At the sound of the trumpet he rears his heroic head back, laughing in the face of fierce adversity. The warhorse, devouring the distance with rage, runs on to meet the armed men. He gallops into the clash of battle. He mocks at fear and is not the least bit intimidated. Retreat is never an option, so he never turns back from the surgical sharpness of the sword. As he fights, the blowing of the trumpet and the beating of the shield and sword do not scare him. The glittering spear thrown within inches of his life does not scare him. The shooting of the arrow en masse does not frighten this horse. What made this horse different from every other breed? He was a warhorse. He was bred to fight. It was in his blood. There is no doubt he was born for battle!

The warhorse is not to be confused with the beautiful stallions that make their residency in the king's stable. These are show horses and for a reason. They are held in high honor because of their exquisite detail. The tone of their muscle is simply breathtaking to the human eye. Their hooves are manicured with precision and inlaid with gold. Every hair on their gorgeous body has been combed and cut to perfection. Precious jewels have been interwoven throughout their long radiating mane and tail. They are escorted by their trainer down the long runway, and the elite crowd is ecstatic with shouts of praise. The beauty of these beautiful animals beggars description. They shine like a rare cut ruby set on a snowy white cloth. They are such an artistic and rare breed that they have no equal on the show floor. However, to ride these horses into battle would be as foolish as attempting to cross the Devil's Triangle in a canoe. For at the first sound of the trumpet they would turn and run just as fast as their golden hooves could carry them back to the king's stable. The clashing of the sword and shield would bring more distress than one could imagine. The show horse is absolutely worthless in the battle. Why? Because it is not in their blood. They were bred for another purpose—to show—and not to fight. You can always recognize show horses by their attitude. They will be there as long as they are in the spotlight. If you put them on stage or on display, you can count on their participation. However, if you fail to mention them by name or accidentally overlook them in the process of commendations, they will forever be offended. If there is no publicity, they just are not interested because they live and operate with one motive, the applause and accolades of others.

Jesus admonished us not to sound a trumpet like the hypocrites do when we give an offering. Then Jesus reveals their humanistic motive: "That they may have glory of men." Jesus added: when you pray, don't give a big song and dance to attract the attention of everyone around you like the hypocrites do; but, rather, enter into the secret closet and shut the door because God sees in secret and He will reward you openly, (Paraphrased) (Matthew 6:6-18). God is in need of war horses not show horses. The warhorse fights as long as he lives, and he lives for the battle until every drop of blood flows out of him onto the battlefield. If we seek our crown in time, we will lose our crown in eternity. Jesus told the Church at Smyrna, "Be thou faithful unto death, and I will give thee a crown of life," (Revelation 2:10). At the judgment, the Lord will not be looking for awards, trophies, and medals. On the contrary, He will be looking intensely for the marks, cuts, bruises, and gashes you received while fighting this good fight of faith. Paul declares in humiliation yet as a proud soldier, "For I bear in my body the marks of the Lord

Jesus," (Galatians 6:17). The word "marks" is another word for scars. A scar is the lasting evidence that somewhere in the process of life you received a wound. Most of the scars we bear in our bodies were produced because of our own foolishness. A drunken fight, careless driving, not paying attention while operating power equipment. But as a soldier of Jesus Christ, like Paul, we ought to bear in our lives His scars. Scars we have received on the front lines of spiritual battle. Instead of being marks of shame they ought to be badges of honor. Like the Purple Heart Medallion awarded to the soldier wounded in combat. Scars become the decorative symbols of conviction and courage.

After the battle, the warriors returned to their camp, and personally cared for their faithful horses, removing the bit and bridle, the armored saddle, and sweat-soaked blanket. They meticulously examined the horses' bodies, pouring in oil and wine and binding every open wound. Though this mighty creature of God's creation was scarred, wounded, and weak, because of the special care it received, it would live to fight another day.

Suffering and scars are a necessity in life. There is no way you can avoid them. Suffering is as unavoidable as bones at a chicken dinner. Jesus is the best man the world has ever known, and He is the best man the world will ever know, yet Jesus suffered. He was born to die for the sins of the world and that came with a price tag of suffering. Everybody suffers according to Job: "Man that is born of a woman is of few days, and full of trouble," (Job 14:1). One of the devil's biggest and most believed lies is that only the good people suffer. But that is not true. Evil people suffer too and probably worse; their suffering has brought them abused bodies, hardened consciences, built-in suspicions, and aging before their time. No one in this life escapes suffering. There are only three kinds of people on planet earth: 1) A good man, 2) A bad man, and 3) A God man. And they all three suffered that day on Calvary. So, since you must suffer, suffer...

> trying to live a better life,
> > trying to be a better Christian,
> > > trying to rear your children in the fear of the Lord,
> > > > trying to make this world a better place to live.

You can suffer trying to be a good soldier for Jesus Christ; and, when you suffer for Jesus' sake, you don't mind the suffering, and you don't mind the pain.

As you read these words, you may be in the fight of your life, and retreat stands as an ever present possibility. The enemy screams at you just to give up, lay down your sword, and surrender to your circumstance. But get a second wind and determine within your own heart you are not going to retreat, retire, or run away. Come heaven, hail, or high water you are going to fight because you were born for battle; it's in your blood. Live and fight in the spirit of John Paul Jones, who helped our nation secure its freedom during the Revolutionary war. The French king lent Jones the *Bonhomme Richard*, which Jones had renamed after *Poor Richard's Almanac*, in honor of Benjamin Franklin. On the 23rd of September, 1779, Jones engaged the British frigate *Serapis* off Flamborough Head, Yorkshire, under the light of the moon. *Serapis* was a superior ship compared to *Poor*

Richard. She was faster, more nimble, and carried a far greater number of eighteen pounders, forty-four cannons in all. The two ships shot simultaneously at one another. At the first or second salvo, two of Jones' eighteen pounders burst, killing many gunners and ruining the entire battery as well as blowing up the deck above. After exchanging two or three broadsides and attempting to rake the *Serapis'* bow and stern, the commodore estimated that he must board and grapple, a gun-to-gun duel seeming futile. During this stage of the bloody and desperate battle, *Serapis'* Captain Pearson, seeing the shambles on board *Bonhomme Richard*, asked if the American ship had struck, in other words, "Are you ready to give up?" Jones stood on the bow of his burning, sinking ship and framed his immortal reply that most any American can quote verbatim, "I have not yet begun to fight." It served as a rallying cry to the crew. The two ships grappled and Jones relied on his marines to clear the enemy's deck of men; and, they did. *Poor Richard* sunk but John Paul Jones and his men sailed out on their new ship, the *Serapis*. When you are in the heat of battle and every odd is against you and the subtle enemy of your soul offers you compromise in the form of surrender and says, "Are you ready to give up?" stand flatfooted on the Word of God, throw your head back, and shout, "Ha, ha, I have not yet begun to fight!" Devil, you haven't seen anything yet!

You may be small in stature and weak in limb, but, when you fell down at the cross and accepted Christ's atoning sacrifice, you gained all access to the power of God as it is written, "You have overcome: because greater is he that is in you, than he that is in the world," (1 John 4:4). You are welded to the throne of God, and there is no way hell can knock you out! You have overcome, so don't throw in the towel or jump overboard. You are a winner by the grace of God.

On New Year's night, 1865, in Nashville, Tennessee, General Scolfield was leading the mighty Northern armies. They were making a push that could have possibly ended the Civil War in thirty days, and for a while it looked as though he would succeed. It was bitter cold that evening as the sun sat behind the wasted clouds. The snow was falling, and the ground was frozen. The Southern army was in rags. They were hungry, their guns frozen to their hands. General Hood was trying to lead them that night for he knew, if the line broke, the South was lost, and General Lee wouldn't make it in Virginia. All of a sudden the muskets began to crackle; the musket balls were spinning off the frozen ground. You could hear the grown cries of the dying and the wounded. Hood was trying to rally his men when suddenly the lines broke. The boys in tattered gray threw down their broken muskets breaking ranks to run. They were whimpering and crying, "It's hopeless. The battle is lost." Suddenly, riding a snow white horse, that great cavalry chieftain, Nathan Bedford Forrest, raised a sharp saber in his hand and began to ride those battle lines that night, the musket balls clipping the buttons from his coat while the cannon shot burst about his head. He just raised his sword and screamed that rebel yell. There beneath the glare of bursting cannon shot they saw this mighty warrior, and they rallied to him and re-formed the line. And with human bone and human flesh they stopped the North's mightiest army—Scolfield's best. Many years after that night in Nashville one of those old war veterans was interviewed. His back was bowed and bent with age. He walked with a limp. His hair was white from the snow of many winters. When they asked him of that memorable night on the battlefield, his eyes flashed. He said, "Oh, I was there that night in Nashville. It looked as though we had lost, so we broke ranks and ran. But when we turned back we saw our great general standing in the face of the enemy. I will never forget Nathan Bedford Forrest riding those battle lines oblivious of fear and death. I will never forget Nathan Bedford Forrest with that sword in his hand. I will never forget Nathan Bedford Forrest standing there in the very brunt taking the best the North had. And we saw him, rallied to him, and we held them that night in Nashville. That night General Nathan Bedford Forrest rode into my heart and he rides there still!"

Many years ago as a mixed up teenage boy on my way to hell, I lost hope in life, and I couldn't find anything to live for. I was threatened by doom, darkness, devils, and damnation. My life was reduced to a perpetual party which, in short, was a life without substance. When it looked like all was lost and I would be swept aside in a maelstrom of iniquity. In January 1980, on a Sunday night, I was at a friend's house at a small party and there on the coffee table was a Bible. I picked it up, then turned to the book of Revelation, Chapter 20, Verse 6:"Blessed and holy is he that hath part in the first resurrection: on such the second death hath no power, but they shall be priests of God and of Christ, and shall reign with him a thousand years." For the first time in my sixteen years of living I heard the voice of God speak to my heart. He said, "If you will live for me, you will reign with me not just a thousand years but for eternity." Then, I heard His voice for the second time say, "Tonight I am calling you to be a soldier. Follow me." I'll never forget that night so long ago, the night General Jesus rode into my heart. Since that time, I have faced everything hell has had to offer, and I am still standing because I'm not going to stray far from His side. That night General Jesus of Glory rode into my heart, and He rides there still!

Chapter
11

An Old Habit That Can't Be Broken

Now when Daniel knew that the writing was signed, he went into his house; and his windows being open in his chamber toward Jerusalem, he kneeled upon his knees three times a day, and prayed, and gave thanks before his God, as he did aforetime.

Daniel 6:10

*A*bove everything that could be said about prayer, I believe I am safe in saying most people want their prayers answered. Who is interested in just praying prayers for prayer's sake? Only a Pharisee prays to appear religious. I personally do not pray to be seen or heard of men. I pray to be heard of God. Discipline or Christian duty has nothing to do with it. Prayer to me is coming in contact with the living God and finding the answer to life's most confusing questions and sometimes I need an answer now.

A missionary was chased through the jungle by a large ferocious lion. The lion finally cornered him. With no chance of escape, the missionary fell on his knees and called out in prayer. To his unexpected surprise the lion suddenly fell on his knees and began to pray. "Praise God, it's a miracle," said the missionary. "When all hope was gone, God touched the old lion and he is now joining me for prayer." To that the lion replied, "Would you please shut up and quit interrupting me? I'm saying grace."

Problems have a way of eating you up. My problems have never stopped to pray for me but rather prey on me. Peter said, "Be sober, be vigilant; because your adversary the devil, as a roaring lion, walketh about, seeking whom he may devour," (1 Peter 5:8). It is in those times you need a connection, you need an answer. God ever stands ready to show Himself strong if you will pray. The atheists have a new dial-a-prayer. When they call it, no one answers. Not so for the child of God for He gave us this iron-clad guaranty, "Call unto me, and I will answer you, and show you great and mighty things, which you don't know," (Jeremiah 33:33).

The Apostle Peter was cast into prison with no hope for escape "but prayer was made without ceasing of the Church unto God for him," (Acts 12:5). The angel was dispatched from the sacred precincts of eternity winging his way through the ionosphere. He arrived within the confines of an old Roman prison house. There the man of God was asleep, bound to two soldiers. The angel smote Peter on the side and said, "Get up preacher, I'm busting you out, we're having a jail break tonight." And the chains fell off his hands and he was set free. This is a direct effect of the prayers of the Church; they made prayer.

Sometimes you have to make prayer. Prayer doesn't always come easy. There are those times you have to work, stretch, and sweat. Before the fall of man, prayer came easy. It was just a matter of walking with God through the cool gardenia garden. But after Adam sinned he was pushed into a world of thorns and thistles and the curse was to work the ground by the sweat of his brow. Before this he never broke a sweat: no work, no weeds, no mess. But after the fall, he was thrust into a world of hard labor and he had to contend with spiritual forces when it came to prayer. The New Testament puts it in terms we all can understand, "For we wrestle not against flesh and blood, but against principalities, against powers, against the rulers of the darkness of this world, against spiritual wickedness in high places," (Ephesians 6:12).

The Old Testament calls it travailing in prayer, comparing it to the process of giving birth; that process is traditionally called travailing. On the norm women don't go to the delivery room with a six-pack of Dr. Peppers, a jumbo bag of barbeque chips and a box of Moon Pies, because it is not a picnic; it's more of a battleground. Women go expecting work, sweat, tears, and pain because unless they travail, they will die in the process of childbearing. Unless the church travails in prayer she also will die in the course of giving birth.

Modern science has tapped into a whole new dimension of power; it's called atomic power. It has been here since the creation, but it took many years to finally touch it. There is a whole new dimension to your life in prayer if you will take time to pray and seek God. The power of prayer has also been here since the creation, for Adam walked and talked with God in the cool of the day, but very few really tap into its potential. Prayer is as vast as God and as far-reaching as eternity. We miss so much because we do not pray. Books on prayer are good, but unless prayer is made books are as useless as cookbooks are to a starving man. You can starve to death sitting on the front steps of a restaurant, clutching a book on cooking. You can read a library of books on prayer, but in order to tap into the explosive power prayer you must pray.

How can we expect God to be present in our prayers if we ourselves are absent from them? If you had a calf tied to your back porch, and every time you prayed you fed the calf, how long would it be until that calf was ready for the market? The prophet Daniel knelt down three times a day to pray and give God thanks. The Bible says he did this every day. Daniel had a habit he could not break. His habit wasn't smoking, gambling, or watching porno on the Internet. He had a habit of praying! His habit was seeking the face of the living God. Daniel was addicted to praise and thanksgiving.

Addiction has people in its control the length and breadth of this spinning globe. Sad to say, the Church is not exempt. The body of Christ is not without its fleshly compulsions. Yet, if more Christians would get hooked on prayer there would be less bondage in the pew. Many live a double life and have asked this question a thousand times, "Can I be free and live a normal life?" The answer is as close as the knees on your legs. It starts down on your knees in prayer. When you feel the drawing obsession, open your prayer window, get down on your knees, and cry out to almighty God! It is just that simple. There is really nothing complex about it; just pray.

Mrs. Colman's kindergarten class went to the local fire station on a field trip. The fireman was instructing them on what to do in case of a fire. He said, "Go to the door and feel if it is hot." The next instruction was "Fall on your knees." Then he posed a question: "Does anyone know why you should fall on your knees?" One little fellow said, "Yes, sir, I know. So you can start praying to God to get you out of the mess." When the fire of desire burns too hot, it's not time to give in and submit to the flesh. Fall on your knees and ask God to get you out of the mess!

You must form a habit of prayer in your life. Habits aren't formed overnight; they take years. One Beverly Hills physician told a famous Hollywood actor, "You have to quit taking those sleeping pills every night because they are habit forming." The star replied, "Habit forming? Don't be crazy, Doc! I have been taking them for twenty-five years."

A chain is built one link at a time. Have you prayed today? Don't let another day go by without praying. Is it possible that you have lived on God's grace without gratitude? Do you breathe His air, eat His food, and enjoy His sunshine, and yet not stop just to say, "Thank you"? Even a dog of the lower nature will lick your hand when you feed it. If we declare our dependency on God's loving grace the very least we can do is stop and say, "Thank you, Lord."

The word "habit" means "to hold" or "to fit." It is used to indicate either a way of living or the process of breaking in new clothes. Both are much alike. A coat or a pair of shoes creases and wrinkles to the form of its wearer. An old coat fits better than a new one any day of the week. There comes a time when the wearer says, "This suit fits well." Praying is not always easy; however, if you will practice it long enough there will come a day that it will fit well. Prayer adjusts to your lifestyle and you will become a man or woman of prayer instead of someone who just prays prayers.

In my observation, all people pray in times of danger or emergency. During the tornado that hit Oklahoma City in 1999, my brother Tim and his family found themselves huddled in their bathroom. Outside the twister was unleashed with a vengeance, bent on death. The brick was somewhat beat off their house. Twisted boards slammed through their ceiling. The chimney was thrown to the ground like a rag doll. Cars and trucks were flying and smashing into houses all around. During this living nightmare my brother and his family were not Christians (I am proud to say they have, since then, given their hearts to Jesus Christ), but they were praying. We called them after the phone lines had been restored. My sister-in-law Shelly told my wife, "I prayed and preached better than Guy ever thought about!" Tornados have a way of making people pray. Sickness, surgery, drought, and death have a way of making people pray. In times of emergency we all pray our best and most desperate prayers.

Three men were discussing the best position to approach

the throne in. The first man said, "On your knees is by far the best position, for it shows your unworthiness." The second man said, "I believe being completely prostrate on your face is the best way to pray. It really proves the humbleness of your heart." The third man casually replied, "The best position I have found is upside-down in a post hole all night." In the face of sudden danger people pray instinctively to God. I believe it is a defense mechanism that the Creator placed within the soul of man. Just as instinctively as the goose flies south for the winter, or the squirrel stockpiles nuts high up in his oak penthouse, the soul of man prays when faced with spontaneous endangerment.

The Bible says Daniel "prayed aforetime." If in your life you have formed the habit of prayer before the crises, you can meet every plight and perplexity with an amiable calm. If you will pray aforetime nothing will take you from behind. The sudden assault of the enemy will find you with your armor on, sword in hand ready for battle. When you face "the valley of the shadow of death," which we all will, you can find blessed assurance as you lean on your faithful and familiar Shepherd. There is a peace that passes all understanding for the person who lives a life of prayer. It's much like preparing for retirement. If a person waits until that golden day it stands to reason it may be too late. You must start young and let compound interest work for you. And if you have, when that long awaited day comes, you'll have more than a gold watch and a useless plaque, all because you were ready aforetime.

Jesus spoke a parable of a wise and unwise builder. I believe Jesus called the unwise builder "foolish." He built his house upon the sand, unlike the wise builder who built his house upon the rock. The rain descended, and the floods came, and the winds blew, and beat upon both houses. One man was ready aforetime and the other man was not. The man that was not, his house fell with a great crash. Paul said in 2 Timothy 1:12, "For I know whom I have believed, and am persuaded that he is able to keep that which I have committed unto him against that day." That day I will be ready. Sadly, many people have become very cynical about prayer and praying, even to the point of unbelief. They don't believe prayer will solve any problem. They blame God, the church, the preacher, anyone they can find to pin the fault on. They say, "We prayed but nothing happened." But many prayers fail to enter heaven for the same reason a whole generation of Israelites failed to enter in the Promised Land— because of unbelief. There are some things that are your responsibility in answered prayer. One thing is certain: you can't treat God like a spare tire and pray only when you get in trouble. Bear in mind that you can pray when you get into trouble, but prayer is so much more than that. The three keys to answered prayer are simple:

1 God says, "Need Me"
2 God says, "Listen to Me"
3 God says, "Obey Me"

The decree went out: There was to be no prayer for thirty days. If you were caught the punishment was the den of lions, a sure and certain death, not to mention a terrible way to die. Those vicious, starving man-eaters paced back and forth, driven by a biting hunger, and anticipating the taste of human flesh and blood. With eyes aflame they awaited their prey. A very important point normally goes unseen to the casual Bible reader. Daniel was not thrown into a lion's den, but rather into a den of lions. There is a well-defined distinction. A lion's den could have as few as one lion. Realistically, a lion's den could have no lion present within. It would be my professional advice to anyone contemplating going into a lion's den to wait until the lion is gone. Make sure that no one is at home. However, a den of lions indicates that more than one lion is present in the den. The den that Daniel faced was full of lions. But it takes more than den of hungry, flesh-eating lions to keep a praying man from praying. The Prophet couldn't even put his prayer off for thirty days; but some Christians haven't prayed in thirty days.

How important is prayer to you? Is it a habit worth dying for? When Daniel knew that the decree was signed by the emperor, he went to his house, knelt down at the open window, and prayed to God as he had always done. Literally, it was death for a prayer. If the federal government passed a law restricting prayer for the next thirty days, with the sentence of death as punishment, would you pray?

Nathan Hale, the great Revolutionary War patriot, was captured and hung by British soldiers. His now famous final words were, "I only regret that I have but one life to lose for my country." He was willing to die for his nation and its freedom. During the final days of World War II, it was apparent that the Japanese were fighting a losing battle, yet, many of their pilots, dubbed "kamikaze," willingly flew suicide missions. There was great honor in dying for a cause.

The pilots were willing to die for glory. People are willing to die for that which is of great importance to them. Prayer should be that important to us.

Prayer must become the driving force of your life. Of course it's not so much the method of prayer as it is the addiction to God's presence. Don't be guilty of desiring God's presents rather than God's presence. Prayer has got to be more than just trying to talk God out of something. Yes, I believe prayer can do anything God can do but the main objective to prayer should be to be in fellowship with God. Dust and Deity mingled together. I don't envy the man who only wants a wife just to do the laundry, cook the meals, iron the clothes, feed the dog, wash the kids, and take care of him when the lights go out. It's not going to be marital bliss around his house. If you want heaven and not hell, you must want your wife for who she is. God is no different. We have made praying nothing short of a SOS to God until we're seeking things under the pretense of seeking God. Jesus Christ is interested in meeting your every need but it is only after desire for Him has been established. When the addiction is for His person, you have all access to answered prayer. In short, quit seeking the gift and start seeking the giver because when you have God's Son, you have all God possesses! It's then you can boldly enter into the throne of grace and see the miracle of answered prayer.

Several decades ago in the city of Chicago a miserly old woman lived. She had been very successful in real estate, buying low and selling high. Within one of her business transactions, she purchased a large building at a very minimal price. It was put on the market immediately with a price tag of ten thousand dollars. She told her selling agent not to budge one penny. After a few days she contacted her agent to inquire about any leads. The agent said no one was interested except one man, a preacher named D.L. Moody. He wanted to buy it and convert in into an orphanage. The funny thing is, after he was told the price he offered one thousand dollars. The lady immediately sprang to her feet and slammed her scrawny little hand down on his cherry wood desk and shouted, "Well, did you sell it to him?" He replied, "Why no, his offer was ridiculous." Then he added, "Besides that, you gave me strict orders not to reduce the asking price not one penny." She looked at him with a penetrating eye and said, "You find him tomorrow and you sell it to him for a one thousand dollars." The agent said, "But, I don't understand." The old woman said, "It is easy to understand. I know that preacher D.L. Moody, and he knows God, and he knows how to pray, and when he prays he'll get it for nothing!"

There is just something to be said about a man or a woman who knows how to pray. Daniel knew very well how to pray. Do you know how to pray? It could save your life and it will save your soul. The time is now for every blood-bought child of the King to open their window, get on their knees, and pray to the God of Daniel. Cry out to the God of Abraham, Isaac, and Jacob. His name is Jesus Christ, the maker and the shaker of the universe. Only He has the power to take the bite out of the lion, the heat out of the furnace, the wind out of the storm, the demon out of the man, and the man out of prison!" I think it is time to pray, and that, my friend, is an addiction you can't live without.

Chapter
12

Faith's Resolve

*If it be so, our God whom we serve is able to deliver
us from the burning fiery furnace, and he will deliver
us out of thine hand, O king. But if not, be it known unto
thee, O king, that we will not serve thy gods, nor
worship the golden image which thou hast set up.*

Daniel 3:17-18

Those three short words, "but if not," serve as a complete and unabridged definition of real faith. This was the conclusion that three Hebrew young men reached at the mouth of a burning fiery furnace many distant days ago. True convictions in life are faced with liability and will always be brought in for accountability. Your faith will forever be assaulted and threatened, for it's not what you say you believe, it is what you believe, the conviction of your heart. In the case of Shadrach, Meshach, and Abednego their faith brought them a crisis. The artist who dips his brush into the paint and with heavy strokes only paints big clear open skies, sun always shining, and birds always singing, hasn't painted the whole picture. In life the sun doesn't always shine and the birds don't always sing. I say that not to weaken your faith, but to give you true perspective, like a compass in the storm.

There is no one on this earth who believes in the miraculous more than I. God has healed my body countless times and not just in simple ways. I was healed instantly of a heart defect that I had received at birth. The Lord has gotten me out of more things than I have time to write. My daughter Shanta was healed of Juvenile Rheumatoid Arthritis, better known as J.R.A., a crippling disease with no known cure. So I believe in deliverance, miracles, and the power of Jesus Christ. But the question still stands: What do you do when the healing doesn't come? After you have prayed, and even fasted, and the answer is as far away as when you started, what then? When you stand at the grave of the one you loved more than life and you just knew God was going to show up at the last minute, but He didn't? Will you cast your faith aside and discard it like a fairy tale or will you stand flat-footed on God's unshakable foundation and shout faith's resolve "But if not—!"

The king asked the question, "Is your God able to deliver you from the fiery furnace?" The answer came: "Is the Pope a Catholic? Does a one-legged duck swim in a circle? Do two rattlesnakes kiss with caution? Of course our God is able! What kind of God do you think we worship? Our God is abundantly able to deliver us from every furnace in life. There is no question of His ability or power. We serve the only true and living God who has all power to do more than your little micro brain could ever imagine. However, that's completely up to Him. And if He so chooses not to, let it be known, O king, we still will not bow to your golden idol and that is completely up to us. We accept the full consequence and judgment of our actions. Do with us as you will for that is completely up to you, but just remember, our faith is resolved and unmovable—live or die, sink or swim, we will not bow! You can count on that! We would rather be thrown into the furnace and die, being reduced to a smoldering ash, than to cast our faith in God aside and live a thousand years in cowardly rejection bound to your every command. We will have no other God before us." The faith that pleases God is a "but if not" kind of faith. Nothing else is faith. The ancient patriarch Job put it this way, "Though He slay me, yet will I trust in Him," (Job 13:15). Forget the furnace! If God Himself chooses to slay me I will still trust and obey. The issue is not the furnace, but it is trust and faith in God.

When my oldest son Silas was about two years old I was attempting to train him in the art of sleeping in his own room. The night was dark and after I had lovingly tucked him into his bed I slowly retreated and got into mine. It looked as though I had been successful when suddenly a little voice broke the silence, "Daddy, I'm scared." I said, "Son, don't be afraid. Jesus is with you." He replied, "I know He is, but I can't see Him." To that I said, "You can't see Him but believe you me He can see you."

Life was so uncertain during the German blitz over England. On a particular night the sirens went off signaling for the Brits to find shelter and then the bombs began to drop exploding with a vengeance, lighting up the city of London like a candle in a fish bowl. A father was scurrying through the streets with his small son looking for a place to hide when they came to a large hole that had been left by an exploding shell. The father hurriedly leaped down into it, then turned to see his son standing at the rim with his little body silhouetted against the burning buildings afraid to jump. He said, "Jump, son, and I will catch you." The little boy replied, "But daddy, I can't see you. It's too dark." The man then said, "Son, I know you can't see me, but I can see you, so trust me, I will catch you." The boy closed his frightened eyes and jumped into the loving arms of an unfailing dad.

Take a calm assurance even in those fearful moments when you can't see Him that your heavenly Father sees you. Yes, there are definite times in your life that you can see the Lord and testify to the evidential fact that He is there. Yet, there are other times it seems as if heaven is a solid sheet of double insulated brass and you can't see God anywhere. It is in those times that faith is purified and just simply comes down to, "but if not." Job cried out in desperation in chapter twenty-three, "Oh that I knew where I might find him! Behold, I go forward, but he is not there; and backward, but I cannot perceive him: On the left hand, where he doth work, but I cannot behold him: he hideth himself on the right hand, that I cannot see him: But he knoweth the way that I take:

when he hath tried me, I shall come forth as gold."

As much as I believe it is the will of God to divinely heal sick bodies, I must admit it doesn't always happen where and when I want. Though divine healing is an absolute in the Holy Scripture, I still can't tell God to do it, I can only ask. Everything is in His providence – it's called "sovereignty." Some of the best saints I have ever known never got healed until they got to heaven. The prophet Elisha was one of the greatest prophets that ever served God, yet he got ill and died. "Now Elisha was fallen sick of his sickness whereof he died," (2 Kings13:14). But I tell you he's not sick now!

My wife's grandmother Mildred Brown was a rose in a garden of weeds. She was, by far, one of the greatest saints that ever lived. Granny Brown developed a tumor on the brain. As a family, we prayed for her healing. It never came on this side of heaven and she died. But her healing did come when God took her home, and she's not sick now!

D.C. Brahnam, my college president, died with lung cancer. He was a man of God, a prince among men. Right before his death I attended a meeting at the college. At least two hundred preachers gathered around and prayed for him while fifteen hundred believers extended their hands and joined in a long, extended time of prayer. He wasn't healed that night, and in a few months he was pronounced dead. But I can tell you that in just a little while I'm going to walk the streets of that world with him and there will be no cancer in the man of God, for the Lord healed him when He took him out.

To say God has to heal every physically ill body on this earth when they pray, and that He really has no choice, is misleading. We ought to pray and believe God for miracles, and never skirt the issue that Jesus Christ came to destroy the curse of sickness; however, to make it a rule of faith that God is bound to His word and He absolutely and unequivocally has to heal every human, or it is a lack of faith on our part, is to build on unscriptural foundation. Paul gave a descriptive account in Hebrews, Chapter 11, of the saints who refused to deny their faith. Many never received their deliverance on earth, but they had faith to live, and they possessed faith to die. "And these all, having obtained a good report through faith, received not the promise." Their resolve was, "We believe our God is able to deliver us out of your hand, O king. But if not, just know this, we believe Jesus is the Christ and He is not just another God to be worshiped with the multiplicity of gods that you worship, He is God!"

For some, it cost them their temporal lives, but they gained their eternal ones. When James Guthrie was led forth to the gallows to give his life rather than his faith, he was given one last chance to renounce the Lord Jesus Christ, to which he gave this stirring reply, "I durst not redeem my life with the loss of my integrity." He lost his life, but he gained a new one. What about the prophet Jeremiah? What author or noted speaker can articulate the agony that he endured the last few fleeting moments of his life? He was sawn asunder. History records that the Apostle Peter was crucified upside-down because he felt unworthy to die in the same manner as the Lord. Peter had more victory upside-down than most people have right-side up! Time would not allow in the telling of John the Baptist, of James, of Matthew, of Savonarola, or the many saints who went to heaven on wings of smoke and fire. O, yes, I know our God can deliver us, "but if not." Everyone wants to go to heaven but who is willing follow in the footprints of the Savior? "Then said Jesus unto his disciples, If any man will come after me, let him deny himself, and take up his cross, and follow me," (Matthew 16:24). Are you willing?

There are always two sides to every coin, yet we have developed a mentality as faith people of what I call a one-sided faith. We only see faith on the side that looks good and feels well. Rightfully so, as we are human and have every desire of a fallen species. Since we were kicked out of Eden we have been trying to get back, whether consciously or subconsciously. Only a deranged mind indulges in pain for pains sake. Christ came to redeem the whole man, but like every other promise, it has conditions, and timing has everything to do with it. One man put it this way, "It is always the will of God to heal but it's not always in His wisdom." I can not teach and believe faith is the way out of all my problems. My faith is not hinged upon what may, or may not happen to me. It is not founded upon what may, or may not have happened to the one I love. It stands on this blessed and glorious fact, God! Anything outside of God is a fool's religion. There has been more than one multitude follow Jesus of Nazareth for the fishes and the loaves only to walk away whenever great demands were place upon them, such as a cross. Real faith cannot be preserved with a materialistic guarantee.

I believe God wants to heal you. But if He doesn't, will you still serve Him? He wants you to prosper. But if you go from riches to rags, do you have an answer? "Naked came I out of my mother's womb, and naked shall I return: the Lord gave, and the Lord hath taken away; but blessed be the name of the Lord?" If life doesn't work like you had planned, and all you have after a life of sweat and hard toil is the broken glass of vanquished dreams, can and will you still believe? Be careful you don't get too attached to this world and ground your faith in its foundation. I remind you "that the world passeth away, and the lust thereof: but he that doeth the will of God abideth forever," (1 John 2:17). The possession of your faith is more valuable than all the gold that is stockpiled at Ft. Knox; than all the oil in Texas; than all the coal in Kentucky; than all the diamonds in South Africa.

The devil is not out to destroy your house, your car, or your bank account; he is forever scheming to destroy and take your faith. He may use certain elements or points of contact to get at your faith. But when your faith is built on nothing less than Jesus blood and God's righteousness; if all you possess is gone tomorrow, you can stand and shout, "On Christ the solid rock I stand, all other ground is sinking sand." When you have nothing left but God, you have enough to start over again.

According to I Peter 1:7, our faith will be tested and by fire "That the trial of your faith, being much more precious than of gold that perisheth, though it be tried with fire, might be found unto praise and honour and glory at the appearing of Jesus Christ." Fire is a consuming force and has destructive power. But it also is a purifying factor, especially in gold, and as gold is tested by fire it comes out more pure. When your faith is put through the furnace of affliction it will come out refined and purified. As fire reveals the purity of gold, affliction reveals the purity of faith. Gold shines brighter after it's been through the fire because it has been eradicated of imperfections, particles of dirt, and every other tainted, foreign object. Your faith glows more radiant when put through a fiery test because it takes out all the impurities like deceitfulness, pride, bitterness, worldliness, lust, envy, and jealousy, just to name a few. Here is the beautiful thing about it: When you come out of the fire there will be less of you and more of Christ. You will take on a brand new image: the image of Jesus Christ. You say, "I was promised a crown, so what am I doing with this cross?" It's simple! You and I are not ready for a crown; we're not crown material yet. The cross is redirecting us, reshaping us, remolding us, and fashioning us for the crown.

It is said of the royal pristine crown of England that it's only worthy of the image of the Queen herself, no one else. Only Christ's image is truly worthy of the crown of heaven so God must fashion us in the likeness of His only Son, for it is written, "For whom he did foreknow, he also did predestinate to be conformed to the image of his Son, that he might be the firstborn among many brethren," (Romans 8:29).

There is so much more to faith than the temporal near-sidedness that we have thrust our emphasis on. We have been commanded by God to contend for the faith that was once delivered unto us. You and I stand as a gladiator in the arena of battle to contend and protect the faith of our forefathers. If you were to let down the standard and give up this most precious faith, I pray a million ghosts be resurrected from the blood-soaked floors of the Roman coliseums, from the darkened halls of the catacombs, from the mouths of lions, the crackling fires in the gardens of Nero, and thunder those most holy words to you, "Contend for the faith!" And even if He chooses not to deliver, make up your mind and settle it forever in your heart, "I will serve Jesus Christ come heaven, hail, or high water; whatever it takes, or whatever it costs, I will not bow down to any golden image. He has the power to get me out of trouble, "but if not" I will still be faithful." Jesus told the Church at Smyrna in the book of Revelation, "Fear none of those things which thou shalt suffer: behold, the devil shall cast some of you into prison, that ye may be tried; and ye shall have tribulation ten days: be thou faithful unto death, and I will give thee a crown of life."

During the days of Sir Francis Drake many young men sailed with the great captain. One man had the opportunity but declined. Through ingenuity, sweat, and hard work he grew fat, rich, and prosperous. One day word was received that Sir Francis Drake and his crew were coming into harbor. The rich man went out to the dock to greet the sailors. As the men of the sea came, one by one, down the wooden gangplank the rich man recognized a sailor who had been his friend when both were much younger. As the two men met, the rich man said, "Look at yourself! After all these years of sailing you don't have much, do you?" The sailor put down his duffel bag, straightened his shoulders, and with a twinkle in his eye replied, "No sir, I haven't got much in this old world, as you say. There have been times when we were shipwrecked, hungry, cold, and desperately afraid. At times I thought we would never make it back. However, I can say one thing you will never be able to: I have sailed with the greatest captain that ever sailed the seas!" Paul met his destiny on the road to Damascus and it beggared and ruined his every earthly prospect. It left him to stonings, shipwrecks, prison, and death, but he gave this world his creed in Philippians 3:8: "I count all things but loss for the excellency of the knowledge of Christ Jesus my Lord: for whom I have suffered the loss of all things, and do count them but dung, that I may win Christ." Can't you see what he was really saying? "I've lost everything on the voyage, but I have sailed with the greatest Captain that ever sailed the seas of time!"

I pray before this life is over that I'm never sick again, never hungry, cold, poor, or lonely. "But if not" I can say I have sailed with the greatest Captain that ever sailed the seas of time! Together we will sail beyond the vale and will dock in the City of God. Jesus Christ is my faith and to that I am resolved!

CPSIA information can be obtained at www.ICGtesting.com
Printed in the USA
LVOW072135200212

269614LV00001B/168/A